little house in the city

little house in the city

living small within city limits

marc vassallo

The Taunton Press

. . . .

FOR LINDA

 The Taunton Press

The Taunton Press, Inc., 63 South Main Street, PO Box 5506,
Newtown, CT 06470-5506
Email: tp@taunton.com

Editor: Peter Chapman

Copy editors: Valerie Cimino, Ronald B. Roth

Jacket/cover design: Stacy Wakefield Forte

Interior design: Stacy Wakefield Forte

Layout: Stacy Wakefield Forte

Front cover photographer: Borzu Talaie

Back cover photographers: Martin Tessler (house photo),
                                    Ken Shepard (author photo)

The following names/manufacturers appearing in *Little House in the City* are trade-
marks: Airbnb℠, COR-TEN®, Craigslist®, Dodge®, Homasote®, IKEA®, Lego®,
Toblerone®, Volkswagen®, YouTube℠, Zillow®

Library of Congress Cataloging-in-Publication Data
Names: Vassallo, Marc, author.
Title: Little house in the city : living small within city limits / Marc
Vassallo.
Description: Newtown, CT : The Taunton Press, Inc., 2018.
Identifiers: LCCN 2018014596 | ISBN 9781631868429
Subjects: LCSH: Small houses. | City and town life.
Classification: LCC NA7533 .V37 2018 | DDC 728--dc23
LC record available at https://lccn.loc.gov/2018014596

Printed in the United States of America

10 9 8 7 6 5 4 3 2 1

acknowledgments

I could not have made this book—and would not have had half as much fun making it—without the help of many people at The Taunton Press. Thanks especially to Rosalind Loeb, Lynne Phillips, Barbara Cottingham, Jennifer Renjilian-Morris, Stacy Wakefield Forte, and my editor, Peter Chapman, as steadfast on this, our fourth book together, as he was on our first.

This book would not have been possible without the generosity of the talented architects, designers, photographers, and others whose work appears here and the willingness of so many gracious homeowners to share their homes. Heartfelt thanks to my agents, Allison Cohen and Susie Cohen, with me all the way.

Thanks to Bill O'Luanaigh for an early read and for infinite support. Thanks to photographer Ken Gutmaker for the photos of my little house in the city. Thanks to architect Bob Swain for profound inspiration and for lunches at Serafina. *Grazie mille.* Thanks to Stephanie and Sam for two nights at your sweet ADU.

Thanks to all my neighbors, who remind me every day of why I love living in Seattle. Most of all, thanks to my wife, Linda, and our son, Nick, who have helped to make our little city house a true home.

TABLE OF CONTENTS

the next little thing

· · · ·

My house in Seattle is small, just 950 sq. ft., but my home doesn't stop at the front porch or even at the front gate. It includes sidewalk garden beds, the street, the neighborhood, and the whole city, all near at hand.

a change is taking place all across the country and especially on the West Coast, a shift led by the younger generations. People who in years past might have headed for the suburbs are moving instead to the city or choosing not to leave. Most will live in apartments or condos. Indeed, multiunit residential buildings all but define our modern notion of a city. But in cities that have neighborhoods of detached dwellings (and most cities still do), people are buying, building, and fixing up little houses. In West Coast cities—and here I must include the Canadian city of Vancouver, with its stratospheric real-estate market—the rising prices of even the smallest city houses suggest that the demand outstrips the supply.

Many people who already live in a little city house are staying put, remodeling perhaps, but not trading up or moving out. Others are building a little house in their backyard to serve as quarters for guests or extended family, or as a rental home for single people, couples, or small households, or even as an Airbnb for overnight visitors. Rental income helps pay for the little house and ultimately helps offset the mortgage on the main house. A few intrepid souls are finding clever ways to fit a little house into novel spots in the city—building one on the rooftop of a warehouse, or repurposing an industrial structure, or transforming a two-car garage into a home.

Many people who already live in a little city house are staying put, remodeling perhaps, but not trading up or moving out.

why a little house in the city?

Sometimes there's room for a little house on a vacant sliver of city land, as with this narrow house in New Orleans (left), or in an unlikely urban spot, as with this small house on a warehouse roof in Seattle (right).

Cities are growing again. According to the U.S. Census Bureau, 2.3 million more people lived in metro areas in 2013 than in 2012; and in all but five of the fastest-growing metro areas, the largest contributor to growth was people moving in, not babies being born. People are choosing cities for a host of reasons, job opportunities and a desire for cultural richness chief among them. Some are expressing a preference for a life less encumbered by things and a hope (not unfounded) that living in a densely inhabited city will be better for the planet than contributing to sprawl.

Meanwhile, the size of the average American household has declined from 3.01 persons per household in 1973 to a low of 2.54 persons per household since 2013. The aggregate numbers are more telling: Of nearly 126 million households nationwide in 2016, roughly 78 million, or 62 percent, are made up of one or two people, and roughly 98 million, or 78 percent, include three people or fewer.

You could look at these two trends—the growing urban population and the shrinking average household size—and conclude that there will be a whole lot more people living in apartments and condos, and you would not be wrong. Yet many people (and a great

Both this row house in Philadelphia (above, with window box) and this former carriage house in Los Angeles (left) make up for their small size with proximity to transit, schools, parks, shops, and other urban amenities.

many children) will always feel most comfortable with ground under their feet. Humans are hardwired for earth. We're hardwired for fire (the kind you get when you burn wood in a fireplace or stove or outdoor fire pit). We're hardwired for plants, for dirt, for growing things to eat, even if it's just a patch of lettuce or a couple pots of basil. Of course, there will be lots and lots of apartments, but the conclusion I draw is that a great many people will see the appeal of a little house in the city.

In a little house, you'll probably be in a denser neighborhood, so you'll also be closer to your neighbors. I think this may be the best reason of all to live in a little house in the city.

All else being equal, a little house is likely to be less expensive than a larger house. In the city, this means that whatever amount you have to spend on a house, if you put the same amount into a smaller house, you can afford a more advantageous location, closer to downtown, closer to public transportation, closer to walkable amenities such as libraries, shops, parks, and schools. Perhaps closer to all of these. You'll probably be in a denser neighborhood, so you'll also be closer to your neighbors. I think this may be the best reason of all to live in a little house in the city.

a certain kind of conviviality

I want to tell you about my own little city house and why I love it so much, but I can't tell you about the house without also telling you about my neighborhood—in a very real sense, house and neighborhood are one continuous experience.

Our house (shown on p. 2 and p. 9) was built in 1927. It has one bedroom on the ground floor, a second bedroom in a finished attic under a low roof, and one bathroom. It's 950 sq. ft.—on a good day. Bungalow would be far too grand a word for it. It is 20 ft. wide and sits on a 30-ft. by 100-ft. lot. The neighboring houses are 10 ft. from it, not an uncommon arrangement in Seattle. The real estate website Zillow says that it has a fireplace, despite all evidence to the contrary.

In the backyard are two structures we call shed-studios (shown on the facing page and on p. 21). The smaller of the two is 8 ft. by 12 ft. On one end is a small writing table and two bookcases; on the other end are backpacks and snowshoes hanging from nails. The walls and floor are plywood, and the ceiling is covered in weathered cedar boards. A shallow loft holds sleeping bags, tents, and bins of backpacking and kayaking equipment. It's

Our two backyard shed-studios are insulated, finished inside, wired, and heated. They're extra rooms!

my dream come true . . . books and outdoor gear together under one roof! My wife, Linda, uses the larger shed-studio for exercising and practicing Reiki, except when our musician son, Nick, is home, and then he fills it with guitars and amps. He keeps a piano in there, too, as if to prove a point about how much can fit in 120 sq. ft.

We built the shed-studios not because our house has too few square feet but because it has almost no storage space. No attic, no basement, no garage, and just two closets—a small one and an ordinary-size one that also houses the furnace. We also wanted a little more space for writing, meditating, and exercising—activities that aren't always a good fit inside the house. Linda and I agreed that each shed-studio would have to absorb some household items. Thus my hiking boots and favorite books coexist with tax files, old videotapes, and a paella pan too large for the kitchen.

Even with the shed-studios, we don't have a lot of indoor space. What we have instead is a stake in a densely settled, walkable neighborhood of modestly sized houses that's part of a vibrant city, much of which lies within easy reach by bike or public transportation. We

A SMALL DISTINCTION

This is a book about the kind of city house I live in now, a 950-sq.-ft. house in Seattle's Roosevelt neighborhood, 4.41 miles north-northeast of the Space Needle as our resident bald eagles fly. I call my house little, though others might call it large, and who am I to argue? There is no single type or size of city home that's right for everyone, and, anyway, people and households change over time. My dream, years ago, was to live in a yurt, and I may yet. Imagine a nomadic hut in the city! Why not? I may yet live in an apartment.

A few houses in this book are small enough to be called tiny, if by that you mean less than 500 sq. ft. But there's a distinction worth making between tiny and little. Houston-based architect Mark Schatz, whose own house appears in this book, puts it like this: "Tiny houses are about reduction, about paring down to essentials. Small houses are about refinement." I'd have said little rather than small, simply a matter of preference.

For this book, I define little as any house under 1,800 sq. ft.—an arbitrary cutoff, I admit, but one that doesn't seem unreasonable when measured against the median size of a new American home, an astonishing 2,467 sq. ft. in 2015. Several houses in this book are in the range of 1,500 sq. ft. to 1,800 sq. ft. A few, as I said, are less than 500 sq. ft. Most are between 500 sq. ft. and 1,300 sq. ft. In the end, it wasn't a number I was after but a spirit. A sense of littleness. Every house in the book has it.

have a tree-covered playground at the end of our block; raised vegetable beds I built in the median between the sidewalk and the street; fruit trees in our backyard; a community garden across the back alley; and a high school so close we can hear the marching band at practice. We have conversations with neighbors and passersby alike, strings of lights that glow above the backyard fences, grapes that hang into our yard from our neighbor's arbor, and a resident, one-footed crow known to all as Jitterbug. Kids climb the trees along the street, professors bike to the University of Washington nearby, runners and parents with strollers pass through on their way to expansive Green Lake Park, and nearly everyone, much of the time, walks to restaurants, grocery stores, and small businesses mere blocks away. If I ask Siri for a coffee shop near our house, she lists 15 within a mile.

The spot where our little house connects to all of this is our front porch. Thanks to an enlightened former owner, the cedar-clad porch is both wide and deep, proportioned like an outdoor room, and we've furnished it thus. An adjoining cedar pergola, cloaked in a purple-flowered akebia vine, marches past a large, front-facing kitchen window, adding a visual layer to what is otherwise a very simple house form.

When our big dog, Gus, was alive, he sat for hours in a wicker loveseat on the porch, master of all he surveyed. Neighbor kids loved him. Strangers heading to the park fell for him instantly. A woman I didn't know once came up to us during a walk and said to him, "Hello, Jazz Dog!" She turned to me. "I call him Jazz Dog," she said, "because one day I walked by your house and he was lying on the loveseat without a care in the world, enjoying the beautiful jazz music pouring out the front door."

This is what I mean by conviviality. Neighborliness. Liveliness. Warmth. The pleasure of good company. Of course, you can find conviviality in any kind of home in any kind of place. But conviviality has a particular flavor—and perhaps a degree of inevitability to it—when you live in a little house among little houses in the city.

what i look for in a little city house

As nice as it is, our house could be a good deal nicer. We are slowly transforming the kitchen and living room into more amenable and workable versions of themselves, and one day we will punch a door to the backyard, so our covered side-yard stroll will be one of two ways to the patio and the outdoor shower we hope to build. And then there's the flat roof above our bedroom at the rear of the house. Sometimes we look up at the flat roof and imagine a small, modern cube that would be a bedroom with a sweeping neighborhood view. We'd turn our ground-floor bedroom into a study. Other times, we think a rooftop deck would be wiser; certainly it would be less expensive.

Over the years, I've looked for city houses that can teach me something about how I might further transform my own city house and how I might better live in it. Most of the houses I chose to share with you in this book are primary residences like mine. Some were built or remodeled to be rented or to serve as a place for guests or extended family. A few

were set up expressly to be rented short-term, through Airbnb or similar for-rent-by-owner services. I kept rentals in the mix because, to me, that doesn't define a house; it defines a state the house is in. Today's Airbnb might be tomorrow's full-time home. Some of the most inventive new city houses are little ones built for short-term rental, liberated from holding to every domestic convention.

I organized the houses into three groups, which form the three parts of this book:

INFILL: By this I mean a new house built to replace a substandard or derelict house that was torn down, or a new house built on the rarest of finds, an empty city lot (generally one so oddly shaped or constrained by zoning that it had thwarted prior attempts to build on it).

REMODEL: Remodeled houses include everything from a significant reimagining and reconfiguring of an existing little house to little houses with modest additions, small changes, and updates.

ADU: An Accessory Dwelling Unit, or ADU, is a second residence built on a lot with an existing house, typically in the backyard, often oriented to an alley. An ADU can be attached to or located within the main house (such as a basement apartment), but I've selected mostly stand-alone structures. On the West Coast, ADUs are often referred to as backyard cottages, though many aren't cottagelike in style. In Vancouver (where ADUs are abundant), they're called laneway houses. I like the acronym ADU, and I'm pleased to see it moving from urban-planning jargon to more ordinary use.

Regardless of which group they're in, the houses are bound together by qualities of good design, some particularly relevant to little city houses, such as scale, light, context, and flexibility. But when I selected houses to share with you, I had three overarching qualities in mind: thoughtfulness, experience, and delight. These three qualities became my personal checklist, idiosyncratic but not arbitrary. The words themselves don't appear too often because it would be tiresome to repeat them across three dozen houses, but each house in this book resonates with these qualities.

Being thoughtful when designing a little city house sometimes comes down to being respectful, not only of the property the house is on but also of the neighbors and the neighborhood.

The designer/ owner of this ADU in Portland, Oregon, embellished the interior with artful tiles of her own design.

THOUGHTFULNESS

I almost decided to refer to this quality as attention to detail, but it's more than that. Thoughtfulness starts with the conception of the house, in plan and in three dimensions. The compact cottage (above) designed by Stephanie Dyer for her own backyard in Portland, Oregon, appears to be a fairly conventional house, albeit a small one, but what Stephanie accomplishes in 342 sq. is remarkable. Everything is where it needs to be. The tiny first floor accommodates not one but two in-swinging exterior doors without disrupting the living area. Stephanie fits in a full staircase and finds just the spot for a gas fireplace, where it can be enjoyed from the eating nook and felt in the bedroom upstairs. Thoughtfulness matters at every scale, including the smallest. Stephanie designed white tiles for the kitchen backsplash, fireplace surround, and stair risers, and patterned tiles for the floor—little touches that add texture to the life of the house. It all seems so effortless, but it's the result of careful and deliberate design.

Being thoughtful when designing a little city house sometimes comes down to being respectful, not only of the property the house is on but also of the neighbors and the neighborhood. When architects Karl Wanaselja and Cate Leger built an infill house in Berkeley (below), they kept the height of the house to a minimum and canted the roof to allow as much sunlight as possible to reach their neighbor's house to the north. They positioned the house on the lot to avoid disrupting a grouping of tall redwoods growing there, members of the neighborhood long before Karl and Cate arrived. The house shares the lot with the house to the south (a condominium arrangement), and the shared space in between is landscaped thoughtfully and generously, so both households can enjoy it. Even the rain is paid respect, captured in rain barrels or channeled toward the backyard garden and redwoods by the gentle slope of the side yard.

· · · ·

This infill house in Berkeley, California, is sited to preserve a graceful stand of redwoods.

"This house is more than a building," Bob said of his home. "It's a complete experience."

The small scale of the mini-kitchen in this basement ADU is integral to its charm.

EXPERIENCE

I'd like to tell you a story to explain what I mean by the quality of experience. The story takes place in the home of Seattle architect Bob Swain, a little house he calls his urban cabin. As we enjoyed a dinner of local crab cakes, Bob said something about the emotional life of a house that applies, in different ways, to all little city houses that sing to me. "This house is more than a building," Bob said of his home. "It's a complete experience." He went on to talk about indoor-outdoor connections, viewpoints, and moments of vitality and life. "It's not a house designed in plan," he said. "It's not just different spaces for different functions. You get a totally different experience in every single room."

"In plan, we organize function," Bob said. "In plan, we make rooms big enough. But we don't live in plan." He was on a roll. "We live through the birds singing in the garden, the dappled sunlight falling through the windows, the breeze lifting the curtains . . . that's the life of a house."

Earlier, we'd gone down to Bob's basement ADU so Bob could make me a Negroni. Bob swung open a bookcase that moves on concealed wheels to reveal a tight spiral staircase, and we headed downstairs, curving past a window with a view into the understory of Bob's native Northwest garden. At the bottom of the stairs was a passageway to the main space of the ADU, but the passageway was also a mini-kitchen and a well-provisioned wet bar, with pantry drawers and a wine rack fitted under the stairs (photos facing page).

We had gone from the living room to the basement, but it was as if we were moving between worlds. Beyond the kitchen passageway, the living space—though small and simple in plan—continued to reveal secrets. From the sitting area, Bob pointed out a window to a tiny, nodding trout lily growing beneath rhododendrons. The garden, in turn, worked its magic on the room, lending it a verdant hue. I'm not sure I could accurately draw a plan of the basement ADU, but I will never forget looking out at that little flower, the sensation of seeing it at eye level.

. . . .

This walk-out basement ADU offers an intimate connection to the garden, one of many indoor-outdoor experiences to be had in what is a modest-size Seattle house on a modest-size lot.

DELIGHT

. . . .

Small flourishes, interesting materials, and smart details are all the more appreciated in the intimate setting of a little house or from the sidewalk of a pedestrian-friendly city street.

Students of architecture are familiar with a quote attributed to the Roman architect Vitruvius (paraphrased by the 17th-century English author Sir Henry Wotton) that "well building hath three conditions: firmness, commodity, and delight." A building must have the strength to stand up; it must function as intended; and—here is where architecture merges with art—it must attain beauty, or delight. The way I put this last point to myself is that a building has be to able to make me smile. I'm pretty sure this is not what Vitruvius had in mind, but that's what I look for in a house. Not necessarily playfulness or cleverness, but a deep sense of satisfaction, a smile of contentment.

In a little house, where you can do only so much, you still have an opportunity to make one thing or a few things truly delightful. Indeed, you almost have an obligation to do so. Delight might involve a really small thing, like bright screws driven partway into the wall to form raised address numbers on a converted garage ADU in Portland. Or it might arise from the signature move of the house, as it does with the full-glass gable end on a bungalow remodel in Vancouver, an unexpected but delightful twist on the iconic house form. Or delight might come from the very idea of the house. Just knowing that there's a little house called Sky Ranch on the roof of a warehouse in Seattle is cause for wonder. When you actually get up on the roof and see Sky Ranch perched at the end of a long wooden walkway, you feel like a kid again.

economies of scale

ABOVE LEFT: The warmth, human scale, and just plain coziness of this little house in Cambridge, Massachusetts, are a big part of its charm, especially in the context of the city.

Behind every little city house lies the story of how its owners found a way, financially, to build it or remodel it or to buy their property in the first place. Sometimes the financial story is fortuitous and straightforward: A woman nearing retirement after a successful career decides to simplify her life and move closer to downtown. She sells her large suburban home for a gain that has accrued across 30 years of ownership, buys a small city home, and remodels it to fit the next phase of her life. With a measure of restraint, she's able to cover both the purchase and the remodel without taking out a mortgage. A few of the houses in this book have stories behind them not unlike this one.

More often, the financial underpinnings of a little city house involve considerable nuance and compromise. Time and again, as I've listened to people who live in little city houses, I've heard stories along these lines: "When I bought this, it was the cheapest house in the city." "We took a chance on a small fixer-upper in a rough neighborhood; it was as much house as we could afford." "The house wasn't like this 20 years ago; what you see now is the result of small changes over time, as we've been able to afford them." "My mother offered to pay us a little rent for living in the upstairs rooms, money she has because by moving in with us she could sell her house." "We built a backyard cottage for rental income that would offset the mortgage on our house, then decided to live in the cottage and rent the house." "The lot had two small houses on it, so we were able to set it up as a

ABOVE AND
RIGHT: This ADU in
Vancouver, British
Columbia, makes
the most of modest
spaces with color,
texture, and basic
materials, honestly
expressed.

condominium of two units and offer one of the units to our friends; it's the only way it pen-
ciled out." "We wanted to be closer to downtown, so we chose a smaller house." And so on.

I prefer to think of these financial circumstances not as constraints but as opportunities for creative solutions. Most of the little city houses in this book are expressions not
only of good design, not only of the needs and desires of the homeowners, but also
of tradeoffs and financial realities. Economics shape what gets built. The best little city
houses succeed not in spite of this but because of it.

a modest hope for the future

A little house in the city can provide you with something both grander and more precious than square footage: a chance to enjoy an unencumbered home life and an unfettered urban life in equal measure.

My hope is that some of you will decide to move to the city and that you will find or build a little house in a neighborhood that suits you perfectly. I hope that if you live in a little city house already, you will stay in it and make it even better without making it too much larger.

Little city houses have the potential to liberate us. Maybe at last we'll get past the tyranny—built into the way our real-estate market operates—that we should worry as much (or more) about the next owners of our house as we do about what makes sense for us and what makes us happy here and now. With the growing likelihood that there will be a buyer out there with a small household and their own reasons for wanting a little house in the city comes the freedom to buy or build your own little city house and to make it into the kind of home you want it to be (within the bounds of what you can afford). The next owner will do the same, and the next owner after that. Houses change. Neighborhoods evolve.

Go ahead and install an outdoor shower on the roof deck. Add that bedroom cube. Build an ADU in the backyard. You'll be glad you did, the market just may reward you, and your city will be the better for it. ▮▮▮

INFILL

designer
HOMEOWNERS

location
PORTLAND, OREGON

one room for two

LEFT: It may be just one room, but it vaults up to a 13-ft.-high wall of windows that looks out to the patio and backyard garden. There's enough height for an extra row of kitchen cabinets, perfect for things you don't need every day.

ABOVE: If the interior of the house is defined by being a single space, the exterior is defined by its simple, sheltering roof. The 8-ft. overhang is sized to block the summer sun and let in the winter sun (which does make appearances in Portland).

Several things appealed to Lily and Jamie about the property they bought in North Portland. The lot was three-quarters of a block deep; the existing house was small and run-down; and—the clincher—the lot had a north-south orientation, with the house squished up on the north end. This unusual arrangement would allow them to replace the house with a simple one that would fit their lifestyle and have a wall of windows facing south onto a large backyard garden. Next came the questions: Did they really want to constrain themselves to the original footprint of the house? Could they fit everything they needed into 704 sq. ft.? The answers turned out to be yes and yes.

There was no question that they wanted their new house to be just one room (with a closet and a bathroom). "Small rooms connected by hallways that seemed like wasted space didn't feel like the right direction to go in," Jamie says. Lily and Jamie's preference for an open, one-room plan had a practical side as well. Between them at the time, they had four big dogs. In the first house they shared, all six family members seemed always to want to be together in the same place; they found themselves choosing this little room or that little room, to no one's satisfaction.

An IKEA bookcase divides the one room into a living space, seen here, and an entry area and home office on the other side. The sleeping nook has room for a dog bed, so that resting pooches can hang out with Lily and Jamie or keep an eye on the backyard.

There was also no question that Lily and Jamie would design the new house themselves and do a lot of the building as well. They'd worked on houses before, and they're problem solvers by nature and training, Jamie as a paramedic, Lily as an experimental physicist adept at dismantling and repairing complex microscopes. They tinker, and they learn by taking things apart or by reading and watching YouTube videos. Yet they weren't averse to hiring help when needed, and, much to their delight, they found Portland's building department to be a willing partner, even with many of their untraditional ideas.

The house Lily and Jamie created has all the space they need in an affordable and energy-efficient package. They have no mortgage; their roof

. . . .

BELOW LEFT: To the left of the front door is a tidy home office for two. With the chairs rolled away, there's room for a workout. Tucked out of view are yoga mats, kettlebells, and suspension training straps.

BELOW RIGHT: The front door is screened by bamboo planted in aluminum stock tanks. A scupper channels rainwater from the shed roof to the bamboo, but most of the rainwater is directed into a 550-gallon plastic cistern just beyond the planters.

"We liked the idea of being together in one space . . . and that our dogs wouldn't have to choose between hanging out with mom or hanging out with dad."

—Lily, homeowner

captures rainwater for their yard; they heat the house with a modest amount of wood; it doesn't take them much effort to keep it all neat and tidy. And so they have time. Time to walk to coffee shops and restaurants; time to garden; time to sit in the backyard and read; time to bike and kayak and enjoy the outdoors, in their city and in the wilderness that lies not far beyond it.

Living in one room isn't always ideal. "When we both work at home," Jamie says, "and we happen to have conference calls at the same time, and it's winter,

Lily and Jamie did not neglect storage space in the design of their one-room house. Inside, a walk-in closet has room for all their clothes and a stacked washer/dryer. Outside, two sheds at the back of the yard hold bikes, tools, and outdoor gear.

and one of us can't be outside, that's a challenge." They've opted for neutral colors so that everything will go together, which means Lily had to give up her favorite bright red carpet. But neither Jamie nor Lily can think of much more than that in the way of issues.

In keeping with their can-do spirit, when they discover that something they originally built isn't quite right, they change it. And they're still coming up with new ideas to try. As Lily puts it, they're still turning to each other and saying, "You know what would be cool. . . ." Building a house is a process, she says, not a one-time event. ▥

architect
RICK AND CINDY BLACK
ARCHITECTS

location
AUSTIN, TEXAS

living small
in austin

Some 15 years ago, Austin architects Rick and Cindy
Black received a call from a friend in the city's North Loop
neighborhood who said, "I have this weird little lot next door
with a tree on it. You guys might want to take a look." Look they did,
and what they found was a leftover bit of land at the inside corner
of a diagonal crossroads. The trapezoidal lot was so small and oddly
shaped that no one had ever built on it. Across the street were the
beginnings of a small park, newly planted with young trees. Intrigued,
Rick and Cindy researched the neighborhood plan and discovered
something called the Small Lot Amnesty rule, which, in the name of
greater density, allows houses to be built on certain undersized lots.
The ruling applied. Rick and Cindy bought the lot and built a house on
it—their first design for themselves—and they've lived there ever since.

A neighborhood of modest, working-class bungalows, North Loop
has become increasingly popular for its quirky shops and vibrant
restaurants and bars. It wasn't always thus. For decades, Austin's airport was located so close by that North Loop was known as the place

"North Loop is full of 1,100-sq.-ft. houses built in the 1930s . . . so we felt like we were on board with the neighborhood's ideal."

—Cindy Black, architect and homeowner

· · · ·

ABOVE: Built on an odd-shaped half-lot that had been passed over for decades, the house enjoys an open setting across from a park. It's 1,090 sq. ft., but from a distance it seems larger because you read it as two separate volumes.

LEFT: Rick and Cindy thought about shaping the house to fit its trapezoidal lot. Instead, the house is a less expensive, more efficient box, and the carport responds to the odd shape of the lot, jutting from the house at a rakish angle.

over which planes lowered their landing gear. In 1999 a new airport was built farther from the city and the noise abated. North Loop still has a coffee shop called The Flightpath, just down the street from the trapezoidal lot.

Rick and Cindy's house—artful and human scaled—fits right in. The Small Lot Amnesty rule capped the size of the house at 40 percent of their lot size, or 1,305 sq. ft. They fit what they needed into an efficient, two-story box, 21 ft. by 28 ft., but the house is anything but boxlike. There's a little cutout for the front entry and another cutout upstairs, between the bedrooms. In plan, the house is divided roughly in two down its length. On one side are the dining room and living room downstairs and the two bedrooms upstairs. The other side is further divided by the staircase, an entry vestibule, and a

. . . .

ABOVE: Rick and Cindy appreciate the human scale of bungalow windows. These windows have modern details and large panes, but they're roughly the size of the double windows typical of bungalows, with windowsills similarly just 2 ft. from the floor.

RIGHT: There is no drywall in the house. Rick and Cindy prefer shiplap boards, typical of 1930s houses in Austin. The cheap, D-grade pine they use takes paint well and results in a clean look, but with texture.

. . . .

LEFT: Shiplap board walls make it easy to hang shelves and fixtures and to reconfigure them when necessary. Open cabinets allow for more efficient storage and fit the casual feel of the kitchen.

BELOW LEFT AND RIGHT: More like a room than a hallway, the open space at the top of the stairs has a desk alcove, laundry nook, and open closets. The second floor began as master suite; a porch was later converted into a child's bedroom, but there's still no door to Rick and Cindy's bedroom.

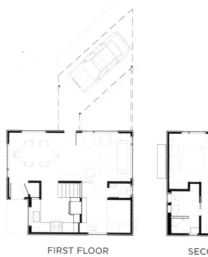

FIRST FLOOR   SECOND FLOOR

powder room, leaving 6 ft. 9 in. of width for the kitchen and a study—not much,
but enough.

The entire upstairs was conceived of as a master suite, though after Rick and
Cindy's son was born, they enclosed the porch and turned it into his bedroom.
Inspired by designers Charles and Ray Eames's mid-century house, they organized
the upstairs so that you move through a functional hallway, passing a laundry
area, closets, and the bathroom, before reaching their bedroom. Rick and Cindy
describe the house as "at once cozy and grand." One big reason for the grandness
is the generous upstairs "hallway," an airy space with room for yoga or quiet time
at the desk alcove.

About that study. At 6 ft. 9 in., it's just wide enough for a queen-size daybed
with storage under it. In theory, it's a guest room, but in actual use it's where the
family hangs out and watches TV or where Rick plays his trumpet. "It's cozy," Cindy
says, "but everyone loves it." She might have said: "Everyone loves it because it's
cozy." In a way, she could have said the same about the whole house. ▌▌▌

reuse house

. . . .

A curved roof lowers both the actual and apparent height of the house. Curved walls create a dynamic experience, particularly in the narrow gap between the two houses that share the property.

In designing and building their own house on a small lot six blocks from downtown Berkeley, architects Cate Leger and Karl Wanaselja were thinking infill, small, and green from the start. They experimented with unusual, salvaged materials, achieved a remarkably high degree of energy efficiency, and created a 1,140-sq.-ft. house that uniquely expresses their innovative spirit and passion for low-impact city living.

The house's siding materials—poplar bark shingles and metal shingles fashioned from the roofs of junked cars—catch your eye, but no less so than the house's curves. Karl can expound on the practical and aesthetic benefits to the shape of the house—honoring setbacks, maximizing sunlight, capturing rainwater—but he allows that he loves curves and had always wanted to design a curved house. "I think that was really the primary driver," Cate says, acknowledging, not apologizing for, the delight they both take in the result.

Guests who arrive at the house, which is just 14 ft. wide in front, tend to be surprised upon entering at how large and open the interior feels. The effect is like that of the charmed tents in the Harry Potter films, which are impossibly larger inside than they appear from the outside. Cate talks about the notion of "borrowed space" as a way to make a small house feel larger. For instance, the area dedicated for dining is quite small but doesn't feel cramped because it borrows space from the kitchen and living room. The

"When you build small, you're using a lot fewer resources and a lot less energy for heating and cooling. . . .The challenge is to do it in a way that isn't cramped or unpleasant, but is an exciting and wonderful experience."

—Cate Leger, architect and homeowner

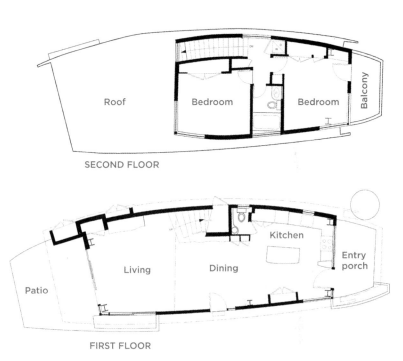

SECOND FLOOR

Roof   Bedroom   Bedroom   Balcony

FIRST FLOOR

Patio   Living   Dining   Kitchen   Entry porch

. . . .

ABOVE: The awning above the second-story front deck is fabricated from salvaged Dodge Caravan side windows. Caravan windows were chosen because junked windows from this popular minivan are readily available.

LEFT: The lower walls of the house are clad in poplar bark shingles, a waste product of the furniture industry. The upper walls are sided with car roofs in shades of gray, painstakingly gathered from local junkyards and cut into shingles resembling fish scales.

entire ground floor feels larger because the ceiling slopes up to 12 ft. high in the living room, where tall windows pull your eye toward the backyard.

Cate and Karl would not have been able to afford the house were it not for favorable zoning conditions and a smart approach to building and financing over time. The 1920s bungalow that came with the property was, in Karl's words, "a total wreck." They bought it because it was on a lot zoned for two houses with only one house on it—which meant there was room for an infill project. They started with a green remodel of the bungalow, moved in, and then built a studio in the backyard from a shipping container. Next they

In keeping with the honesty of the house, the steel moment frame (required to provide lateral stability during an earthquake) is fully exposed. The dining area is small but borrows space from the kitchen and living room.

designed and built the infill house and legally converted the two houses into condominium units. Finally, they sold the bungalow unit to pay for the infill unit.

Cate and Karl's daughter, a high-school student, has walked or biked to school since kindergarten, and Cate bikes religiously, often pulling a trailer of groceries behind her. Karl's mother lives nearby in a green, mixed-use project that Cate and Karl's firm developed. Yet there's always something greener to strive for. Karl recently installed 20 salvaged wine barrels, hooked up in a series, to collect rainwater. Cate, for her part, was recently appointed to Berkeley's Energy Commission, expanding her green-building focus to the entire city. III

LEFT: This delightful bedroom for a teenager doesn't stand on tradition. It has a prominent position at the front of the house, with access to a balcony by way of a bookcase that doubles as a step.

BELOW: A frosted-glass partition wall defines an entry area at the front door, so you're not stepping right into the kitchen. A micro-size powder room is tucked under the stairs at the back of the kitchen, preserving the openness of the main space.

BOTTOM: The ceiling slopes up to 12 ft., drawing your eye beyond the tall windows to the backyard. An open staircase further enhances the feeling of spaciousness.

grade house

· · · ·

LEFT: For all its obvious differences, Grade House fits the scale of the street. Because it sits on grade, not perched atop a partially aboveground basement like its neighbors, it has two full stories yet stays within the height limits mandated by zoning.

ABOVE: Placing the house on grade allows space to flow through the house from the front yard to the backyard. The juxtaposition of the metal-clad white box against the dark stucco breaks down the house volume into a primary and secondary form, reducing its visual weight.

When a landscape architect and a physics professor contacted architects Piers Cunnington and Clinton Cuddington of Measured Architecture to design a new home in East Vancouver for themselves and their young children, they had two wishes at the top of their list: The house had to be built on a strict budget, and the ground-floor living space had to have a strong connection to the garden. The couple wanted their house to be modern but also scaled appropriately for the neighborhood.

To keep costs in check, Piers, who served as lead designer, created a house with a small footprint, an open plan, a simple form, and a palette of basic materials: standing-seam metal and stucco cladding, aluminum windows, and polished concrete floors. But the biggest cost saver was a slab-on-grade foundation. According to Clinton, there's a misperception that what's in the ground is the cheapest part of the house. In fact, he says, digging and pouring a

The staircase is a sculptural element, bathed in light from a skylight above the second-floor landing. There is structure in place to allow added stairs to continue up to the roof, where mountain views await.

"Our clients carefully considered the space they needed . . . opting not to build the maximum allowable floor area for the lot, a move distinctly against the norm in Vancouver, where property values are astronomical."

—Piers Cunnington, architect

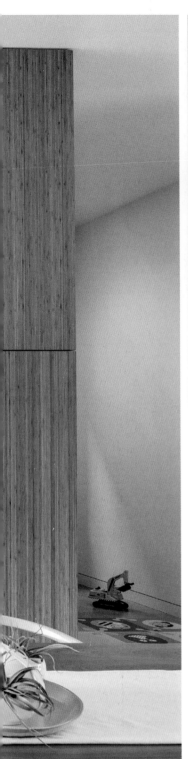

FIRST FLOOR   SECOND FLOOR

. . . .

ABOVE: "The construction process involved ongoing edits to ensure that only elements essential to the design were included," says Piers. In the kitchen, a troweled concrete floor and clean-lined, carbon-ized bamboo cabinetry —at once simple and elegant—made the cut.

basement can eat up one-third of the budget. If you're trying to maximize square footage on an expensive city lot so you can maximize the sale price, you would include a basement. But this house had to make sense only for the clients themselves. Going with a slab-on-grade—getting rid of the cost of a dig and of concrete and steel—freed up the budget.

Keeping the first floor just above grade strength-ened the connection between the interior of the house and the garden. Avoiding a partially aboveground

ABOVE: Just off the kitchen is a small apselike space, tucked away from the larger congregational space but still connected. It's a play area for now, but it could become an office in the future, or perhaps a hangout spot for the family dog.

ABOVE RIGHT: Grade House follows a classic small-house paradigm of packing service spaces—front and back entry areas, stairs, powder room, mechanical room—in a narrow band on one side, leaving the largest possible remaining area as open living space.

basement—typical in the neighborhood—also meant that the two-story house would stay within mandated height requirements and fit the scale of the street. Although the house is fundamentally of a different massing and form than the neighboring houses, it has, Clinton says, "the same visual weight as a traditional home in the neighborhood."

The ground floor is divided into two sides, clearly reflected in the form of the house. The service side—kept as narrow as possible—includes an entry area, stairs, boot room, mechanical room, powder room, and closets. The wider side is open living space with the kitchen as the epicenter, "the new hearth," as Clinton calls it. The upper floor is the private arena: children's bedrooms to the street; master bedroom to the quiet backyard; stairs, bathrooms, and laundry area—less needy of air and light—in the middle.

With budget in mind, Piers conceived of the house in phases. The initial phase involves a fairly bare-bones interior and a yard that can be transformed over time by the landscape architect homeowner. There is structure in place so that one day the staircase can be added onto, taking another turn and rising up and onto the roof. The flat roof would then become a private garden, a "backyard in the air," Clinton calls it. Something to look forward to. ▌▌▌

architect
THE MILLER HULL
PARTNERSHIP

location
SEATTLE

sky ranch

. . . .

Building a little
house on top of
an old warehouse
required the addi-
tion of structural
elements below
the roof to support
the extra weight,
but the result is
magical.

ask Tom what he likes about living in an 800-sq.-ft. house on top of a warehouse in Seattle's Ballard neighborhood, and he answers without hesitation: "The isolation, no neighbors, the quiet." Tom has lived in many houses in his lifetime, most recently a 3,500-sq.-ft. house. Those days are behind him. Or, you could say, below him.

Tom is of an age when one might think of retirement, but instead he has an enviable balance of work and life. He happens to be president of the company that owns the property that includes several warehouse buildings, a marina, and, of late, his house. Two or three days a week, he takes the bus to his downtown office. The rest of the week he conducts business from a dockside office with a view of his rooftop aerie. He enjoys alone time up there, but he also enjoys visitors (he typically throws a key down so they can let themselves in). And he takes advantage of shops, restaurants, and a Sunday farmers market a few blocks away.

When Tom called architect Scott Wolf of The Miller Hull Partnership with his idea for what became known as Sky Ranch, he'd discovered that zoning allowed for a caretaker's unit on the property. He could be the caretaker, he

45

. . . .

The house is perched on the south side of the warehouse. To reach it, you enter on the north side of the building, climb dedicated stairs, and walk across the roof on a raised boardwalk. It's a delightful stroll, but you can't blame Tom for rigging a pulley system near the house to hoist up his daily newspaper.

reasoned, and put the caretaker's unit on the roof. He'd always wanted to live in a loft; here was his chance.

The request was so unusual that Scott at first wondered if Tom was serious, but soon Scott and Miller Hull embraced the challenge. They quickly realized the roof of an old warehouse can't support the weight of anything extra. As Scott says, half jokingly, a pigeon landing on the roof changes the load calculations. Two questions drove the design process: How do you support the house? And how do you get up to it? The answers were a significant (and not inexpensive) structural retrofit below the house and an extension of an existing stairway up to the roof.

Arriving at the basic plan of the house was less involved. The maximum size for a caretaker's unit was 800 sq. ft. For efficiency and cost, Scott went with a rectangle 40 ft. long by 20 ft. wide. He aligned support spaces like a bathroom and walk-in closet in a narrow bar to the north, where the

The sweeping roof overhang is made possible by trusses that run the width of the house. The depth of the trusses determined the thickness of the prominent roof. The overhang shelters a wide deck that extends the living space from inside to outside.

RIGHT: A thick bookcase wall separates support spaces (entry, bathroom, closet, laundry, mechanical) from living spaces. The hearth separates the living room and kitchen from the bedroom, though the bookcase leads your eye past the hearth partition, creating a feeling of openness.

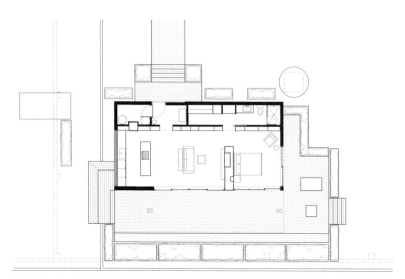

FLOOR PLAN

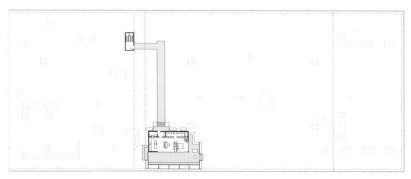

ROOFTOP PLAN

"I have worked with homes and with warehouses, but this was an unusual opportunity to bring the two together."

—Scott Wolf, architect

. . . .

ABOVE: The kitchen is more a pause between the outside and the living area than a room, a flowing effect enhanced by hiding a small refrigerator under the countertop. There's something delightful about the interplay of the books and the wall oven. No need to draw a hard line between cooking and living spaces.

immediate view was of the roof, and the living spaces to the south, open to big views and sunlight. Packing small support spaces into a dense bar or core to keep the living spaces open and free-flowing is a tried-and-true way to organize a house, one that is especially well suited to small houses.

"It is what it is," Tom says of his simple house. "I don't wish it to be larger." Tom speaks with modesty, and his quiet disposition is reflected in the house. Or perhaps it's the other way around. **|||**

architect
KYRA CLARKSON ARCHITECT

developer
MODERNEST

location
TORONTO, ONTARIO

house 1

· · · ·

LEFT: House 1 exemplifies a welcoming modernist aesthetic. The dark siding recedes, lending the house a quiet presence on the street. The natural fir vestibule adds warmth and contributes to the domestic feel of the house.

ABOVE: The house is exactly 14 ft. 10½ in. wide, the absolute maximum allowable on the lot. Architect Kyra Clarkson welcomes constraints like narrowness. "If we didn't want constraints," she says, "we'd be artists."

a rchitect Kyra Clarkson and her husband, planner Christopher Glaisek, started MODERNest to fill what they saw as a gap in Toronto's housing market for small, efficient, well-designed modern houses at a midmarket price. MODERNest is a hybrid firm that combines development and architecture, taking projects from the purchase of a city lot through to the sale of a new home. The idea is to create turn-key city houses for people who don't have the time, budget, or inclination to commission a custom-designed home themselves. Kyra and Christopher imagined a home buyer much like themselves: a couple wanting to raise a family in a vibrant Toronto neighborhood with good schools, good parks, and easy access to transit.

Their first project—called simply "House 1"—was MODERNest's proving ground. Kyra and Christopher needed an inexpensive lot for their model to make financial sense, and they found what they were looking for in a tiny lot in a funky, up-and-coming neighborhood east of downtown. Kyra designed a house that would meet MODERNest's criteria and also fit the neighborhood. She thought a lot about its scale and massing, how

· · · ·

TOP: A large, frameless skylight spans much of the second-floor hall, making it appear almost as though there is no roof above the walls.

ABOVE: The master bedroom captures MODERNest's dictum of "getting the basics right." It's a simple room, well proportioned and crisply detailed. The large window offers a calming view of a 100-year-old ash tree in the backyard.

RIGHT: Clear glass panels allow light to reach the first floor and help to visually connect upstairs and downstairs.

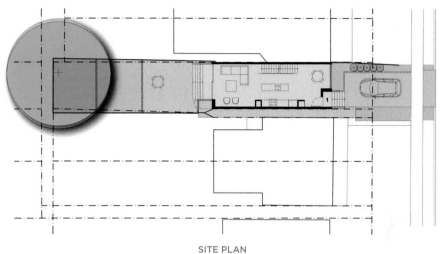

SITE PLAN

"Toronto is a fantastic city where you really can live downtown and take public transit . . . but building yourself a modern house is a huge project."

—Kyra Clarkson, architect

to position, shape, and detail the house so it wouldn't stand out. She wanted House 1 to be unabashedly modern, but also "simple and under-stated." As she always does when designing an infill house, she talked with the neighbors about her plans. Because House 1 would be built from lot line to lot line (all of 14 ft. 10½ in.), Kyra needed the approval of the immediate neighbors, which she received.

House 1 is 1,260 sq. ft., plus a 600-sq.-ft. basement. In plan, it's beautifully straightforward. The main floor is entirely open but for a kitchen island of IKEA cabinets and a short wall of IKEA cabinets book-ended by a small front entry closet and walled-in mechanical chase that matches the look of the closet. Upstairs, there's a bedroom on either end and a third squeezed into the middle. The rooms are clean and

. . . .

In the narrow interior, design is a game of inches. The kitchen island is 2 ft. wide and just 3 ft. from the wall counter and the staircase. The glass panels contribute to an open feel, but they were also chosen because they're just ½ in. thick.

simple, with the master bedroom window and a large skylight above the stair hall framing views of a 100-year-old ash tree in the backyard.

As a modern city home and as a means of establishing a design language for MODERNest houses going forward, House 1 is a success. But it didn't turn a profit. Location really does mean everything. Those who could afford House 1 wanted to live closer to downtown; those who wanted to live in the neighborhood needed something less expensive. Since then, the value of House 1 has risen with the desirability of the neighborhood, and Kyra and Christopher have refined their formula.

The couple has now completed four MODERNest houses in Toronto. They live in House 4 themselves, and they're building House 5 and House 6. It feels like the start of something. Imagine what Toronto might be like someday when MODERNest is up to House 101. ▮▮▮

architect
OJT

developer
CHARLES RUTLEDGE AND OJT

location
NEW ORLEANS

narrow in new orleans

· · · ·

The shape of the house reflects the spaces inside and a desire to present a single story to the street. Corrugated metal cladding fits the neighborhood's industrial vibe, while the narrowness of the house and its position flush with the sidewalk are in keeping with the city's historic shotgun houses.

not long after Jonathan Tate started his architectural practice, he struck up a conversation with developer Charles Rutledge about housing in New Orleans. Jonathan and Charles bemoaned the trouble they and their friends were having finding a house in the city that was priced within their reach as young professionals. No one, it seemed, was addressing the middle of the market between subsidized, low-income housing and the high end. Jonathan and Charles formed a partnership to find that elusive middle ground.

They decided to start in Irish Channel, the historic, mixed-use neighborhood that Jonathan calls home. Prices were rising in Irish Channel as buyers recognized its charms and its proximity to the storied Garden District and downtown. Jonathan and Charles went after 30 nonconforming lots but ended up with just one, a leftover strip of land, roughly 16 ft. by 55 ft., between a Creole cottage and a warehouse. With setbacks, they'd have 468 sq. ft. on which to build. It was an audacious challenge.

The narrow house Jonathan designed is unabashedly modern in spirit. And yet, being long and narrow, it has a clear connection to the

> *"The house is in a transitional area, moving from industrial to residential. It's a nice spot in which to be more exploratory."*
>
> —Jonathan Tate, architect

. . . .

Ample windows allow the textured brick wall of the vintage warehouse next door to be experienced throughout the house. French doors open to a deck that covers virtually all of the Lilliputian 10-ft. by 16-ft. backyard.

one-room-wide "shotgun" houses for which New Orleans is famous. But Jonathan's design departs from a traditional shotgun in two important ways. The rooms in a shotgun are lined up one after the other and separated by walls and doors, whereas space in the narrow house flows freely; the only doors are on the bathrooms. A traditional shotgun is entered from the street; you must walk through every room to get to the kitchen at the back. The narrow house is entered in the middle, with

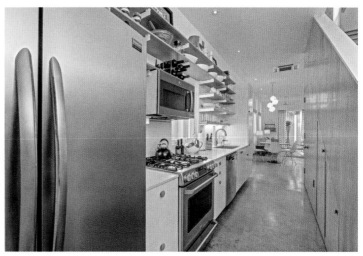

. . . .

ABOVE LEFT: Narrow city houses almost always feel less cramped with windows or doors on the sides, even if neighboring buildings are close at hand. There's only 3 ft. between the living space and the warehouse next door, but those 3 ft. make all the difference.

ABOVE RIGHT: A simple but efficient kitchen is organized along one wall, opposite an oak-paneled staircase with matching doors to storage cabinets and a tiny powder room.

LEFT: The loft adds useful space and gives the bedroom a vertical orientation that makes up for its 10-ft. width. The tall space and high loft window are also great for ventilation. Angling across the space is steel bracing that helps the skinny house resist lateral forces.

BELOW: Jonathan explored many variations of the house in cross-section before settling on the final shape. It's a happy coincidence that the zigzag roofline of the house is in sync with the zigzag roofline of the Creole cottage next door.

ABOVE: Windows on three sides fill the narrow bedroom with light. The placement of the square windows high and low on the wall adds a touch of drama.

RIGHT: The required 3-ft. setback serves as a raised walkway to the house and backyard. A metal mesh security door closes the walkway to the street; the entry door is at the midpoint of the house, just beyond the downspout.

the kitchen to the front and dining and living areas to the back. It may seem like a small distinction, but it makes a huge difference. Arriving at the midpoint, you don't experience the house as being anywhere near as narrow as it actually is.

And narrow it is. At 10 ft. 4 in. wide (measured on the outside), 45 ft. long, and three stories at its tallest, it's a house designed in section more than in plan. Instead of fighting the setbacks, Jonathan embraced them. The slot between the narrow house and the warehouse becomes a raised boardwalk to the entry door and the backyard deck. The sidewalls have lots of windows: small, square ones that peek at the Creole cottage; large ones that capture the texture of the brick warehouse wall.

The narrow house caught the fancy of Holly and Jack, two artists who now call it home. Jonathan and Charles have since purchased half the warehouse and an adjoining vacant lot. They plan to put three units within the warehouse and build nine detached houses mere feet apart from each other on the rest of the property. With the narrow house and their next project, they continue to make good on their economic goal of adding to the middle of the housing market and on a shared aesthetic goal: to put up new houses in an old city that aren't simply replications of what came before them. III

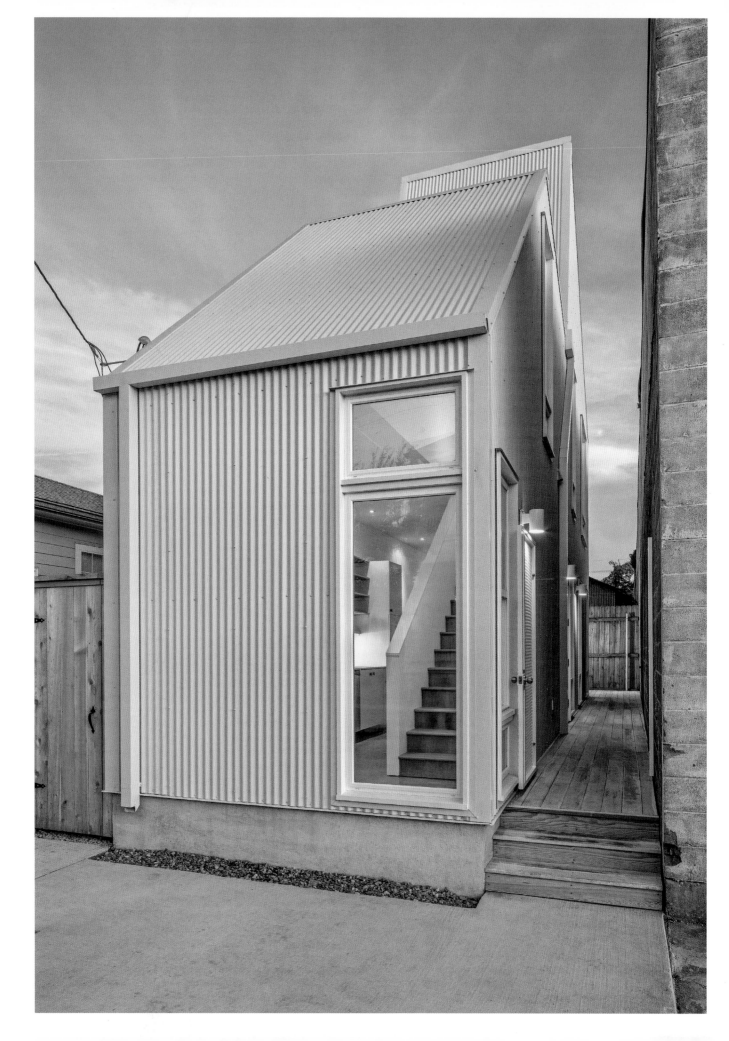

architect
**THAD REEVES, AIA
(A. GRUPPO ARCHITECTS)
AND TKTR ARCHITECTS**

location
DALLAS

inside/outside house

• • • •

LEFT: The soaring extension of the roof overhang gives the house, which might have looked diminutive on the gardened lot, a little presence from the street. The trellis structure hints at the exposed framing inside. And what could be more gardenlike than a trellis?

ABOVE: The pavilion-like house stands in the middle of a 7,500-sq.-ft. lot, which might seem like a farm in some cities but is standard size in Dallas. Under the broad and sheltering roof, the house opens to the backyard garden.

architect **Thad Reeves** calls Little Forest Hills "the most Austin-feeling neighborhood in Dallas," noting its asphalt roads, namesake hills, and old trees. As further support, he can point to a laid-back 1,450-sq.-ft. house he designed while working with Truett Roberts at TKTR Architects, just before he started A. Gruppo Architects. The house so seamlessly blends indoors and outdoors that it's almost an open-air pavilion. It was designed for an empty lot in Little Forest Hills that had been an illegal pot farm, bought on the cheap at a government auction. The clients were avid gardeners who wanted a small house that would maximize the amount of yard that could be gardened. The couple wanted the house to give them the feeling that they were living outdoors. And they had one further stipulation: The house had to be built for an implausibly low price.

By keeping the house to a simple rectangle, roughly 20 ft. by 40 ft., Thad and Truett avoided impinging on garden space, while saving on foundation and roofing costs. The compact footprint also helps foster a strong connection between inside and outside. The first floor is entirely

ABOVE LEFT: The kitchen and dining area open to a walled garden that is both an extension of the interior space and a soft barrier that affords privacy from the street.

BELOW AND RIGHT: A spirit of openness describes not only the flow of space within the house and the connection between indoors and outdoors but also the honest expression of materials: wood framing, steel structural elements, and plywood flooring.

LEFT: The screened porch off the master bedroom feels like a treehouse. Thanks to high ceilings and a sweeping view of the neighborhood, the bare-bones bedroom itself feels like a treetop aerie.

. . . .

ABOVE: With sliding glass doors and a diaphanous wall of translucent polycarbonate panels, the interior seems less like indoor space and more like outdoor space that's been delineated for living but not fully contained.

open, save for a closet and powder room near the front door. Walls of sliding glass open to the outdoors. From any spot on the first floor, you can see into the enclosed garden in front, turn, and see out to the expansive backyard garden.

Every design decision from large to small takes cost into account. The structural system minimizes the use of steel and relies instead on dimensional lumber and prefabricated wood trusses. The exterior is clad with inexpensive panels of cement board and Homasote fiberboard. The pitched roof is covered in standard, three-tab asphalt shingles; a flat roof, though in keeping with the modern aesthetic, would have been much more expensive. The floor on the main level is a basic concrete slab, ground and polished. The couple decided not to finish the ceiling downstairs, to save money and because they liked the look of the exposed joists and fasteners. The floor in the two bedrooms upstairs is plywood, sanded

"When you open up the house, it really does feel like you're in a tent, camping on the property."

—Thad Reeves, architect

• • • •

Given the openness of the house and its compact footprint, you can stand in the backyard garden and see clear through to the walled garden in front.

and sealed with polyurethane. The stair treads are engineered lumber, given the same simple finish. The kitchen cabinets are from IKEA.

And then there's the roof. "It acts like a parasol," Thad says, extending over the house in an exaggerated way, creating shade and shadow, providing protection from sun and rain. With a more typical overhang, Thad says, "it just wouldn't be the same house."

Sadly, the gardening couple split up before construction began; one of them lived in the house for two years before selling it. And yet there's a sweet ending. The buyer turned out to be every bit as much of a gardener. He added decks, extended the garden across the entire front yard, and even started keeping bees. City bees. They make so much honey he has enough to share with his neighbors. III

architect
RZLBD

location
TORONTO, ONTARIO

shaft house

. . . .

Reza screened the front windows with long cedar slats to create some privacy from the busy street, and to distort the scale of the house. Without the usual visual cues, you aren't sure if the house has two stories above the parking space or one double-height story.

a rchitect Reza Aliabadi calls it Shaft House, which is an accurate name for the 1,400-sq.-ft. house he designed for a narrow lot in the East York neighborhood of Toronto. The house is 16 ft. wide on a 20-ft.-wide lot, so its sides must be windowless firewalls. To augment natural light from the narrow north and south ends, Reza placed an open shaft near the center of the house that allows light to fall from a skylight down through the interior. With stairs crisscrossing to either side of it on every level, the light shaft is the dominant element of the house.

And yet Reza could have called the house Staggered House, because an equally defining aspect of the house is its organization on six staggered levels. Each level is a half-flight of stairs above or below the next, and each level is one room (not counting the bathrooms, which are stacked in a solid core). Neither the light shaft nor the staggered levels came about on a whim. Quite the opposite: Each of these elements is a logical and inspired solution to the problem of fitting a two-story house—the maximum allowed—onto a narrow lot at a cost reasonable enough to allow the client, a developer, room for a little profit.

· · · ·

BELOW: Codes that weren't in place when the neighboring houses were built mandated that Shaft House be set well back from the street. Embracing this mandate, Reza detailed the house to visually recede, giving it a quiet presence on the busy street.

RIGHT: The genius of the staggered floor levels is revealed at the back. The half-sunken basement lifts the kitchen/living level out of the ground. Above it, the mezzanine level commands a backyard view. Even with height restrictions, there's still room for a rooftop deck with half-level parapet walls to either side.

It's worth going back to the beginning of the design story to see how each solution led to the next. Toronto has a harsh winter, so to start with, Reza thought he should provide covered parking; he doesn't like the look of garage doors, so he made a pavilion-style parking space. To accommodate the garage, given that zoning only allows for two stories, Reza came up with the idea of staggering the floor levels. There's a basement behind the covered parking space that's half in the ground, with two levels above it (a kitchen/living space and a mezzanine); and there are two levels above the parking space, a bedroom and a master bedroom. The master bedroom sits a half-flight below a roof deck at

"The program for this house is just six staggered rooms. . . . I didn't associate any of them except the kitchen with a specific function. . . . It looks very simple but it gives lots of flexibility to the homeowners to curate their life within the spaces."

—Reza Aliabadi, architect

FAR LEFT: The mezzanine level is the purest example of a room that can be whatever the homeowners want it to be: perhaps a home office, or a sitting area just below the master bedroom, or a playroom a half-level above the kitchen/living space.

THIS PAGE: The open shaft captures light at the roof and sends it deep into the house. The shaft also serves as a visual connector between the half-levels. From the landing outside the master bedroom, the shaft offers a glimpse of the mezzanine and kitchen.

LEFT: Every half-level in the house (except the basement and roof deck) is connected by half-flights of stairs to the levels above and below. From the kitchen/living level, stairs go down to the parking space and front yard and up to the "second-floor" bedroom.

the back of the house, with clerestory windows facing the deck that bring in natural light. In turn, the deck is shielded from the street by the master bedroom.

From start to finish, Reza kept the budget firmly in mind. The house is framed in wood, without expensive steel, and it features lots of recycled materials, including recycled COR-TEN steel on the street front and ordinary aluminum siding on the side walls. But Reza's most important cost-saving move was encouraging his client to buy an unconventional lot, which was purchased for a price far below the average cost of lots in East York. As for the unconventional design, Reza was fortunate to have a client who had studied architecture and was open to new ideas. The great architect Louis Kahn once said, "The room is the beginning of architecture." Without being too grand about it, this narrow little house with its six one-room levels lives up to Kahn's dictum. III

architect
M+A ARCHITECTURE
STUDIO

location
HOUSTON

700-sq.-ft. house

. . . .

The house is a study in three dimensions, a multifaceted sculpture with a roof that curves under a live oak, a little "teahouse" that juts from the roof, and a blue glass cube at the top of the stairs, which Mark and Anne call their "Box of Sky." The exterior surfaces are a mix of residential, commercial, and industrial materials, reflecting the mix of the neighborhood.

In 1994, Mark Schatz and Anne Eamon were architecture students at the University of Houston in search of a place to live. A vacant lot 10 minutes south of the University caught their attention. It backed up to an industrial site, which was a minus, but it had mature pecan trees, which was a plus. The clincher was the price. They bought the 50-ft. by 100-ft. lot through a HUD auction for $2,300—less than 50 cents a square foot.

They built a 200-sq.-ft. garage/workshop on the lot, a base from which they'd build their house, but they ended up living in it for three years while they finished school. During that time they designed a house they could manage to build themselves on a budget they could handle. It helped that Mark knew home construction from having grown up around it.

The house they finished building in 1999 is 700 sq. ft. on two floors, compact enough to fit amid the pecan trees. At the center is a "switch-back" staircase (with stairs that reach a landing at midpoint and then double back). To one side of the stairs are two large rooms: a living/dining room below and a bedroom above. To the other side are two small rooms:

. . . .

ABOVE: The bedroom is 13 ft. by 13 ft., a comfortable size, according to Mark. A rooftop "teahouse," reached by a ladder, extends the bedroom space upward and offers a glimpse of the sky.

LEFT: The translucent clerestory over the dining alcove doubles as a sitting bench in the upstairs bedroom—a reminder, from either room, that there's more to the house beyond the space you're in.

. . . .

LEFT: Rolling bookcases hold a large collection of books in an efficient volume. Side by side, the bookcases form a dense cube that prompts you to see books in a fresh way, much as the compact house prompts you to consider the notion of home in a fresh way.

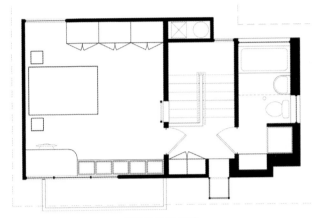

SECOND FLOOR

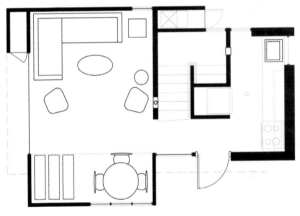

FIRST FLOOR

a kitchen below and a bathroom above. There are some ins and outs to the floor plan, but in essence it's that simple.

The genius of the house is its complexity in three dimensions, the drama of it in section rather than in plan. As Mark puts it, the house "does something different every few feet you slice it." Ceiling heights vary from 7½ ft. to 10 ft.; the roof curves to follow the branches of a live oak tree; and a ladder provides access to a diminutive "teahouse" that sits above the roof like the cupola on a caboose.

"It was really wonderful living in such a nice, small space. I tell people, whether they believe me or not, that it did a lot for our personal relationship."

—Mark Schatz, architect and homeowner

· · · ·

In a small house, even the smallest details matter.

By 2011, Mark and Anne owned two lots adjacent to their first. They had built a 900-sq.-ft. studio for their architectural firm on the original lot and were in the midst of building a 550-sq.-ft. house on the third lot, a gem that embodied lessons they'd learned as practicing architects. (They kept the middle lot as garden space.) With a second child on the way, they knew they would need a little more space, but an addition to the 700-sq.-ft. house wasn't feasible, on aesthetic grounds. "The house is a distillation down to a jewel box idea," Mark says. By adding on, "we'd have so messed up the original." They'd planned to rent the 550-sq.-ft. house to graduate students as an income stream, but they decided instead to add a master bedroom suite to it and make it their new home. So began the next chapter of their adventures in small house living . . . . ▮▮▮

next house

by 2013, **Mark Schatz and Anne Eamon** had spent 14 years living in a 700-sq.-ft. house they'd designed and built themselves (see the previous chapter) on the first of three adjacent lots "inside the loop," as they say of places close to downtown Houston. They'd built a studio for their architectural practice, also on the first lot, and had just completed construction of a 550-sq.-ft. house on the third lot. They chose to keep the middle lot as a garden. The new house represented an evolution in their design and construction ambitions. They called it "Next House."

Their plan was to rent Next House to graduate students to provide an income stream, but with a second child on the way, Mark and Anne decided to move into Next House and add a master suite to it, creating a 990-sq.-ft. house that would work for their young family, which today includes a third child. By doing much of the construction themselves, renting their original house to an employee, and continuing to live on property they own in full, they have been able to set aside funds for raising and educating their three girls.

When you look at Next House, you'd never guess it was two separate building projects; it looks like the two wings were always meant to flank a

FAR LEFT: Mark and Anne conceived of windows not as holes in the walls but as the absence of wall. Windows high and low create different views, depending on whether you're standing or sitting.

LEFT: The distinction between inside and outside all but disappears in the connector between the main building and the master suite.

FLOOR PLAN

narrow courtyard with a pecan tree at its center. Continuity is a big part of the concept for the house. The original 550-sq.-ft. wing contains an open, multipurpose space that is at once kitchen, dining room, and living room. There's an easy flow from this main living space past a functional core (with bathroom, washer/dryer, refrigerator, and mechanical system) to the girls' bedroom and a short connector to the master suite wing.

In the connector, rolling bookcases house Mark and Anne's architectural book collection as well as books for the children. The connector is more than a passageway; it's a quiet place at the hub of the house for pausing to find a book or sitting down to read. Anne likes to start her morning there with the newspaper and a cup of coffee.

LEFT: The master suite gives Mark and Anne some personal space, apart from the living spaces and the bedroom shared by their three daughters. A walk-in closet forms a core that separates the master bedroom from the master bath.

. . . .

LEFT: In the connector between the original building and the master suite are three rolling bookcases, similar to those in the first house Mark and Anne built on the property, but with a greatly improved design featuring metal tracks for the wheels.

NEAR RIGHT: Three young children are a tight fit for one bedroom, but the room has lots of light, high ceilings, and a visual connection to the yard. Plus, the kids have the run of the house—literally, since interior doors are few and far between.

ABOVE: Although it's of average size, the master bath has a rich mix of surfaces, materials, textures, and details. Clerestory windows provide light while maintaining privacy.

LEFT: The house consists of a 550-sq.-ft. original building, at left, and a 440-sq.-ft. master suite addition, at right, with a connector that angles to preserve a pecan tree. The diagonal slate tiles pay tribute to the asbestos shingle siding once found on houses in the neighborhood.

"No matter where you are in the house, you're in the room, you're in the next room, you're in the yard, you're in the courtyard—you're in all these different, visually connected spaces simultaneously."

—Mark Schatz, architect and homeowner

• • • •

High ceilings and a roof plane floating above clerestory windows give the house an expansive quality. The lower height of the kitchen and living room bump-outs (clad in slate tiles) add intimacy and human scale.

Mark and Anne have no regrets that they've stayed put and stayed small. Their little piece of the city is close to downtown, close to the University of Houston, and within walking distance of a light-rail station. There's a bayou nearby with a bikeway along it, connecting Hermann Park at one end with MacGregor Park at the other. Long gone are Mark and Anne's first days in the neighborhood, when they wondered if they'd have to fence their front yard for safety. They never built a fence. Instead, they have fond memories of an elderly neighbor who brought them home-cooked meals while they worked on their house, and dreams of good days yet to come with their three daughters. ▌▌▌

designer and builder
**YALE SCHOOL OF
ARCHITECTURE
GRADUATE STUDENTS**

location
NEW HAVEN, CONNECTICUT

yale building project

. . . .

Exposed on its corner lot, the house has to look sharp on every side. It is modern in detailing and materials (standing-seam metal roofing, clear cedar boards, fiberboard panels) but timeless in form and scaled to complement the older homes around it.

first-year graduate students at the Yale School of Architecture in New Haven, Conn., are given a rare opportunity: the chance to design and build a modestly sized house in an economically challenged city neighborhood. The Jim Vlock First Year Building Project was introduced in 1967; each year since 1989, the program has completed a single-family or two-family house in New Haven. Guided by program director Adam Hopfner and studio coordinator Alan Organschi, the 55 students in the 2015 program designed and built a 1,000-sq.-ft. house in the city's West River neighborhood. The 2015 house is remarkable not only for how comfortably it sits on a challenging corner lot, but also for a design solution so honest, sensible, and (in many ways) universal that it could be transposed to cities far beyond New Haven.

The process by which the Building Project takes students from concept to finished house is no less remarkable than the houses themselves. The design studio convenes in January. Each student designs a version of a house for the chosen site. The class then selects seven or eight designs for further development by student teams. Each team presents its design to the program's nonprofit client, city officials, and the school's faculty and dean. A final design is chosen in late April. The students complete a set of working

The house is not a bespoke piece, tailor-made for a particular person or family. It's designed for a specific site and urban context, but it's also a prototype, not unlike Craftsman bungalows of the early 20th century, a good fit for anyone and everyone.

drawings, form themselves into a construction crew, pour foundations in early May, and then work on the jobsite in shifts through June. A smaller student crew, working as paid interns, continues into the summer, aided by subcontractors on a few tasks. The house is finished and ready to be occupied by the end of August.

Neither the faculty nor the students know who the eventual home-owner will be. The Yale program's client is a New Haven–based nonprofit developer of affordable homes. The city sells a property to the developer for a nominal fee; the students provide the design and most of the

BELOW: The solid core at the center of the house contains all kitchen appliances. Upstairs, the solid core gives way to its inverse, a pyramidal light shaft above an open stairway.

construction labor at no cost to the project; and a number of sponsors contribute funding and materials. The developer then finds a qualified buyer and sells the house at below market rate, with a clause in the deed that prevents the house from being resold at a windfall.

The 2015 house has a dynamic and highly functional cross-section that includes two skylights and a pyramidal light shaft above the stairs, but it is best understood in plan. The first floor is organized around a core that's packed with a powder room, mechanical room, coat closet, and a kitchen wall with all appliances. Pinwheeling around the core is a narrow but thoughtfully organized entry area, a sitting area, and a kitchen space with a long table and an outer wall of low cabinets. On the second floor are three bedrooms and one large bathroom with a stacked washer/dryer, plus a brightly lit space at the top of the stairs with storage cabinets, a corner window seat, and a built-in desk—a highly useful upstairs gathering space you'd be hard-pressed to find in most larger houses.

"When you're designing something and you know the margins are tight, it's a whole different way of thinking. Yet it can still be really great architecture. That's what I hope the Building Project demonstrates."

—Alan Organschi, studio coordinator

On the first floor, a solid core concentrates utilities and mechanical systems while organizing the open space around it.

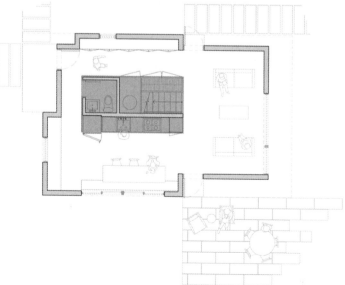

The buyer of the 2015 house is a woman named Jan, a longtime resident of West River who lives in the house with her teenage daughter. Jan appreciates living a block away from the hospital where she works as a teacher at the childcare center. "The house is beautiful," she says. She likes that it's not large; buying it was an opportunity for her to get rid of things she no longer needed. She likes that it isn't expensive to heat. Instead of too many things and too much space to clean, she has time to sit in the window seat upstairs and watch the snow come down, as she did one day last winter. ▮▮▮

• • • •

On the second floor, an open area at the top of the stairs provides space for sitting, reading, doing homework, or simply being together.

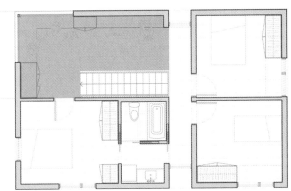

REMODEL

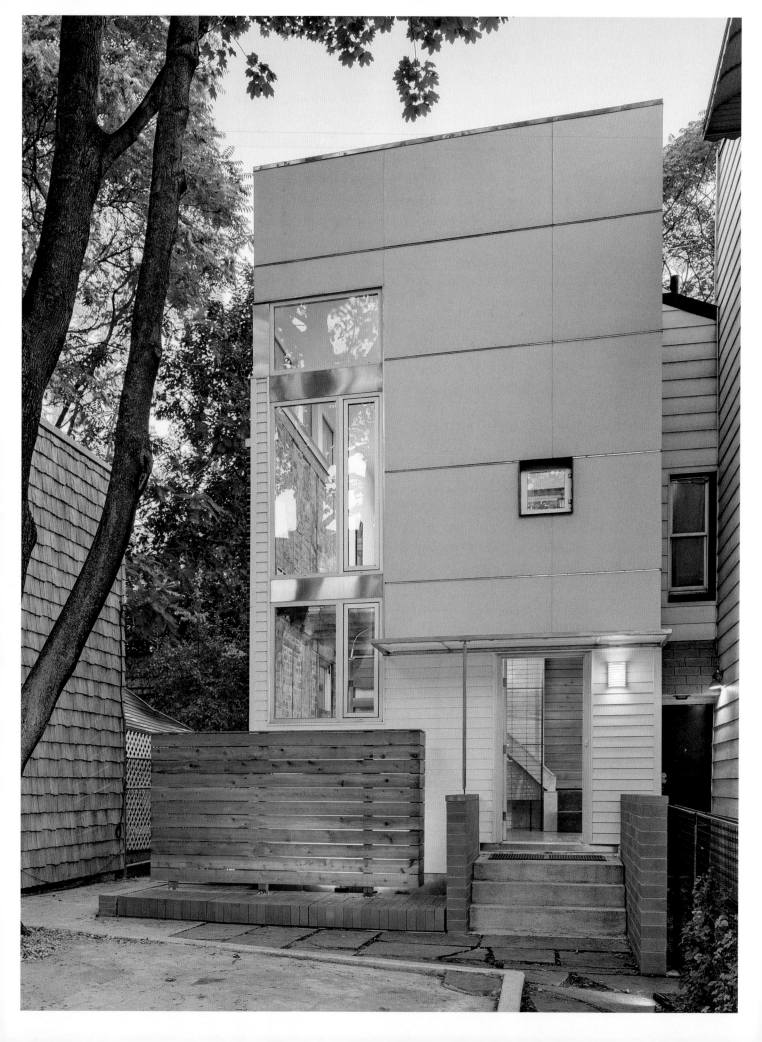

architect
NOROOF ARCHITECTS

location
BROOKLYN, NEW YORK

slot house

· · · ·

LEFT: Scott and Margarita could have added to the house, bringing it out to the street, but they chose instead to honor the 60-year-old maple tree in their vest-pocket front yard. The tall slot of windows offers a view of the tree from both floors of the house.

architects Scott Oliver and Margarita McGrath have something rare in Brooklyn: a row house set well back from the neighboring houses, creating a front yard under a towering maple tree. Although zoning would have permitted them to build out to the street, they opted to confine their renovation to the original footprint of the house and to preserve the tree and the yard exactly as they were. They call their house Slot House, in reference to the tall slot of windows they added to the two-story front facade to allow the maple to be seen from inside. They extended the concept of the slot as they opened up the interior, replacing a slotlike section of wood floor with a transparent steel grill and raising the ceiling height of the second floor to allow for a horizontal slot of clerestory windows along the south wall. And yet a case can be made for calling the house Tree House, in homage to the 60-ft.-tall maple that dominates the front yard and in many subtle ways spreads its influence throughout the interior of the house.

On days when the sun shines through the tall slot of windows, the tree casts its profile in shadow on the birch doors that form a panel behind the staircase, turning the panel into a giant mural. Likewise, the tree casts its shadow on a wall at the center of the main living space. Scott and Margarita assumed that they'd use the wall to display artwork, but when they saw the

Clothes are stored in cedar bins that roll out (like a pull-out pantry) from behind a panel made of stacked birch doors. A wooden ladder leads to a small cellar with just enough headroom to serve as a storage space and laundry area.

dance of shadows, they decided the wall was best left blank, ever ready for the sun and the tree to paint upon it.

The 1,000-sq.-ft. house remains a two-family house, although Scott and Margarita reconfigured the units. At the back of the first floor is a 400-sq.-ft. rental apartment. Scott and Margarita's 600-sq.-ft. unit consists of a room at the front of the first floor and the entire second floor, plus a rear deck that extends over the 400-sq.-ft. apartment. In effect, their unit goes up and over the smaller apartment. Scott and Margarita's first-floor room is

Scott and Margarita conceived of their house as "an open, vertical loft that reveals the archaeology of the original structure." A dynamic mix of solid wood and transparent steel elements animates the interior and allows natural light to reach clear down to the cellar.

"Most row houses have a 30- to 50-ft. rear yard and then they're up at the street. This house is backwards. We have a 30- to 40-ft. front yard . . . with just 8 to 10 ft. between the back of the house and the neighboring property."

—Scott Oliver, architect and homeowner

FIRST FLOOR

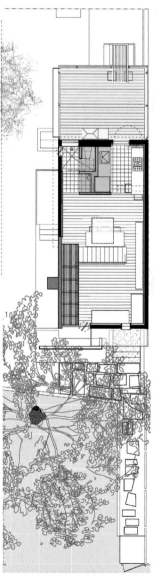

SECOND FLOOR

. . . .

ABOVE TOP: Galvanized-steel stairs rise from the street-level entry area and sleeping space (the bed is visible under the steel grill floor) to the second-story living space. The front-yard tree is visible from the slot of tall windows or from the little square window above the Korean daybeds (a spot preferred by visiting cats).

ABOVE: The white wall at the center of the interior was intended to display artwork, but Scott and Margarita noticed that on sunny days, shadows from the front-yard tree dance upon the wall, and so it has remained a blank canvas for the tree.

ABOVE RIGHT: The minimalist kitchen opens to a deck that sits atop a small rental unit at the back of the house. A steel security grill slides in front of the door to serve double-duty as a ladder to a sleeping loft.

a unique combination of a sleeping area (half-hidden behind a shelving unit) and entry area. The room is dominated by a galvanized-steel staircase that rises behind a steel mesh screen up through the floor framing and onto the steel grill. The loftlike second floor includes a sitting area, a dining area, and a bathroom and small kitchen at the back. Both floors offer a tantalizing blend of new and old materials.

The defining moment of the renovation came early in the project. The contractor had removed all of the finishes, exposing the original brick walls and cedar framing. Scott and Margarita were sitting upstairs on a section of plywood subfloor with their feet hanging down between the beams where the steel grill is now, marveling at the bones of the old house that had been revealed. According to Margarita, "We said, 'Okay, project stop! Let's see how close we can get the final thing to this space right now.'" ▥

designer and builder
REMODEL BOUTIQUE

location
AUSTIN, TEXAS

boutique bohemian

for those with patience and an adventurous spirit but not a lot to spend on a house, it's sometimes possible, even in a city with high home prices, to find a small fixer-upper that's within reach. This is exactly how Kristen and Michelle were able to buy their first house in Austin. It helps that the couple runs a remodeling and construction company called Remodel Boutique, and that Michelle is as adept at building as Kristen is at design. One of the company's mantras is, "Unique spaces should be afford-able by all."

After Kristen and Michelle bought their 952-sq.-ft. house on the East Side, four miles from downtown Austin, they discovered that a drug dealer was living next door. Although a SWAT team made sure he didn't stay long, it was a bit more than they'd bargained for. They didn't mind compromising on the house, but as for the neighborhood, Michelle admits, "We were a little ahead of the curve."

What drew the couple to the 1940s house, besides its reasonable price, was their sense that it had good bones. "We could work with this house without having to change too much," Kristen says. They kept the heart-pine floors, the configuration of two bedrooms with a bath between them, and the clawfoot tub. Pulling down drywall, they discovered burlap stapled to

93

> *"Smallness is a matter of perspective. We lived in a 200-sq.-ft. hotel room for a year. After that, our house felt huge."*
>
> —Kristen Harper, designer and homeowner

. . . .

ABOVE: The welcoming front porch shows what you can do with well-chosen paint colors and a few simple accoutrements. Buying low and remodeling on a shoestring was the only way Kristen and Michelle could afford their first little city house.

RIGHT: In opening up several small rooms into one large room, Kristen and Michelle did not attempt to hide where the old walls used to be. Their honest approach gives the space its rhythm and charm. An eclectic but thoughtful mix of furnishings adds delight.

• • • •

TOP AND ABOVE: The relaxed aesthetic of the kitchen takes creativity and effort but not a lot of money. The 1950s stove is a Craigslist find. Ceilings and floors are original. The painted plywood range hood was built around an inexpensive unit. The butcher block countertops and island are from IKEA.

shiplap pine boards, a sort of homespun wallpaper. They kept some of the drywall, and in certain spots they exposed the boards, which they painted or refinished. They turned the bedroom at the front of the house into a study. In the other bedroom, they solved the problem of no closets with a bank of IKEA wardrobes, one of many places where they mixed vintage and modern.

Most of their remodeling effort involved turning three small rooms into one open living space with a sitting area, dining area, and cooking area. Knocking down walls to make a larger space is a common remodeling move. Less common is the aplomb with which Kristen and Michelle appointed their home with a highly personal blend of old finds, nods to the past, and fresh thinking, all done on the cheap.

Kristen and Michelle, remodelers at heart, have since moved to another house in Austin, larger than their first, but still a little city house. Through their business, they often help young people buy and fix up small houses in Austin. They sold their first house to just such a young family. Their former neighborhood is on the rise. Today you see lots of infill houses and parents pushing strollers down the streets. "It's popping," Michelle says. "It's awesome to be there now." ▮▮▮

bungalow rising

· · · ·

The crisp pediment roof—a modernist take on the Parthenon—meets the historic district's requirement for a traditional, sloped roof, yet it feels current.

the 1940s house that Stephen and Isabel bought in East Vancouver was a bungalow by strict definition (one story, low roof), but it lacked architectural distinction and usable space. With a footprint of 26 ft. by 26 ft., or 676 sq. ft., it consisted of a first floor and a partially aboveground basement, a little over 1,300 sq. ft. total. Both levels were compromised, the basement by a low ceiling and small windows, and the first floor by being an awkward 10 steps above the front yard. Stephen and Isabel were happy to be back in the neighborhood where Stephen had grown up, close to a lively commercial street and a good school for their two boys. But the bungalow was not the simple, open, modern house they had in mind.

Their architect, D'Arcy Jones, saw an opportunity to transform the bungalow into the house Stephen and Isabel wanted by lifting it up and out of the ground. At any given time, D'Arcy has two or three projects in Vancouver that involve a house being lifted in some fashion. Sometimes the house that's lifted is otherwise left exactly as it is. In this case, the transformation was more dramatic, though it's still a remodel that kept a significant amount of the original structure.

Lifting a one-story house to turn a crawl space or (as in this case) a low basement into living space is a cost-effective way to make a small house larger without adding a full second story, which can be more expensive and often exceeds height restrictions.

The house was lifted roughly 6 ft. above the original foundation walls, which were maintained, saving time, money, and resources. The basement was filled with 3 ft. of gravel, and a concrete slab was poured at the grade of the front yard, establishing a new first floor. The numbers are a bit hard to follow, but the result is clear: What had been a dreary basement with a 6-ft. ceiling is now a ground-level first floor with a 9-ft. ceiling and lots of large windows. The new first floor is open except for a small core that contains a powder room, a pantry, and a pocket for the refrigerator. The original first floor is now a second floor with three small bedrooms, one full bath, and a built-in desk at the stair landing. Above the second floor is an office/playroom space within a new gable roof, and here's where things get really interesting.

Living/dining

Deck

Kitchen

Entry

FIRST FLOOR

Master bedroom

SECOND FLOOR

The deep overhang of the gable end accentuates the triangular form of the roof and shields the cedar siding below. The reverse board-and-batten pattern (protruding 2x2s nailed to flat 1x3s) is a nod to picket fences, modern in attitude but with a delicate texture that softens the facade and hearkens back to the bungalow beneath the surface.

RIGHT: Tall windows and floor-to-ceiling doors allow space to flow through the open interior from the front yard to the backyard. A 9-ft.-high ceiling, a polished concrete floor, and minimal furnishings contribute to the feeling of openness.

ABOVE: An efficient kitchen is tucked under the stairs; the refrigerator and a pantry are on the opposite side, set within a solid core that defines the kitchen from the living and dining space. Isabel's father's drafting table finds new life as an eat-in table and work surface.

LEFT: The mix of old and new fir joists supporting the second floor (originally the first floor) rests on the steel beam used to lift the house. "It's beautiful in a blunt way," D'Arcy says. "It's what a farmer would do to hold up the floor."

101

> *"While this house is composed of pure shapes, it has the same visual weight as a traditional home in the neighborhood."*
>
> —D'Arcy Jones, architect

• • • •

D'Arcy calls the third-floor playroom/office the Toblerone room, for the Swiss chocolate that comes in a triangular box. The floor is covered with interlocking rubber mats like you see in kindergarten rooms, which are inexpensive and ideal for absorbing sound.

D'Arcy likens the third-floor space to the long, triangular boxes that Toblerone chocolates come in. At each end of the playroom/office is a triangular wall of windows, with sweeping views of the city and the Coast Mountains to the north. The space is atticlike in form, but it's crisply finished in smooth drywall, without any visible beams, rafters, or collar ties. It's a bit of a visual trick. The sloped ceiling is dropped 6 in. to hide the deep ridge beam that runs down the center of the space, and engineered-steel connections eliminate the need for the horizontal collar ties you often see in attics. The result is a delightfully pure space. It's a jujitsu design move, in a way, to have turned the most traditional aspect of the house—its sloped, gable roof—into its most modern expression. ▌▌▌

row-house update

What you notice upon entering Patricia and Cynthia's mid-19th-century Philadelphia row house is the fresh look and feel of the living area, dining area, and kitchen on the main floor. But in no small way, the remodel hinged on the bathrooms—in this case, the addition of a full bath and a powder room and an update of the master bath. This is not an unusual circumstance in the remodeling of older city houses. The smaller ones especially are quite often challenged in the bathroom department.

The 1,500-sq.-ft. house is in Queen Village, an eclectic neighborhood close to the Delaware River and south of Society Hill, the city's most historic residential area. The house has a front section of three stories, including a walk-up attic, and a narrower, two-story back section. When Patricia and Cynthia hired architects Kevin Rasmussen and Vivian Su, what they asked for was a more open floor plan, a streamlined aesthetic, greater connection between the front and back sections, more bathrooms, and a much nicer kitchen. They had a modest budget and they wanted to stay in the house during construction to save money.

About those bathrooms: The remodel would involve the entire first floor and the only bath in the house, on the second floor. Patricia and Cynthia

LEFT: The 14-ft.-wide row house was built in the mid-19th century in Philadelphia's Queen Village neighborhood, now a favorite of professionals and young families who enjoy its mix of older residences, restaurants, shops, and parks.

BEFORE

Built-in cabinetry subtly defines the dining area and serves as a coat closet for the otherwise closet-less living room. The glass double door in the kitchen and the tall slot window draw your eye to the backyard, expanding your sense of space.

BEFORE

Remodeling the 10-ft.-wide kitchen was a game of inches. The trick was to center the back door between built-ins on two sides. The updated kitchen has a little less floor area but is a much brighter and more efficient space.

planned to live in the third-floor garret with their school-age son. The first thing designed and built was a full bath for the third floor, which would make it possible for the family to stay put during the rest of the project and would ultimately serve the existing third-floor bedroom and a small office space. The master bath would occupy the same generous space as the original bath on the second floor, but it would be the one place where Patricia and Cynthia indulged in nicer finishes and no real compromises. For some owners of little city houses, baths are necessary but no more than that. For others, one large and well-appointed bath can make a big difference in the day-to-day experience of living in close quarters.

And for most, a second bath—often a powder room on the main floor—is a game-changer. As good fortune would have it, opposite the stairs on the main

"Many newcomers to Philly are buying low and making a small house into what they really want. Some are downsizing from the suburbs. Others are upsizing from New York!"

—Kevin Rasmussen, architect

. . . .

The stairs are original, a link to the past, but the landing was reconfigured to better reconcile the change in floor level between the master bedroom in the front building and the master bath in the back building.

LEFT: A full bath (behind the wall with bookshelves) was added to the third-floor garret, maintaining space for a small office. The bath extends over the lower end of the stairwell but leaves enough headroom for the stairs to work.

BELOW: A 2-ft. 7-in.-wide powder room was added where there had been a pocket of exterior space between the front and back sections of the house. In older little city houses, you have to squeeze in bathrooms where you can.

floor was a door to a small outdoor area, notched between the back and front sections of the house. Kevin and Vivian shoehorned a powder room into this pocket of space. Doing so meant giving up a full-size window in the dining area, but by keeping the powder room narrow, they were able to fit in a tall slot window that is a key to the flow of space between inside and outside and the overall feeling of openness in the living and dining areas.

There was talk of an addition to the kitchen, but Patricia and Cynthia nixed the idea for cost and to avoid losing any backyard space. Instead, Kevin and Vivian made the most of the existing kitchen space by centering a sliding glass patio door and placing all of the countertops on one side and built-in storage and a bench seat on the opposite side. The bench seat has become a prime spot in which to sit and look out on the backyard deck. **III**

architect
ANONYMOUS ARCHITECTS

location
LOS ANGELES

eel's nest

. . . .

When Simon bought the property, it consisted of a small, two-story house on a small lot. With no wiggle room and a modest budget, he turned the house into a three-story gem that commands its spot at the end of the street, a mere 10 minutes from downtown Los Angeles.

When architect Simon Storey bought his house in Echo Park, one of the most densely packed neighborhoods in Los Angeles, it was the least expensive house on the market by half. Which is about right for what amounted to half a house: a funky 370 sq. ft. on top of a bunkerlike garage. It was 15 ft. wide, exactly the width of the property.

The surrounding neighborhood emphasizes verticality. There are steep embankments, long concrete staircases climbing between houses, and, across the street from Simon's house, a complex of small, 1920s-era, Mediterranean-style apartment buildings flanking a terraced inner courtyard. The neighborhood feels a bit like an Italian hill town. In this context, it makes sense that Simon would build upward. Given that his entire lot is just 780 sq. ft., he could hardly have expanded the house otherwise.

Working with a very modest budget, Simon reinforced the existing garage, tore down the single story above it, and built two new stories. With the additional story and a rooftop deck planted with thin trees, the house has become decidedly tall and skinny. Simon calls it Eel's Nest, the name given to narrow building lots in Japanese cities. The house is now 960 sq. ft., which is all the space Simon and his wife, Jennifer, feel they need.

109

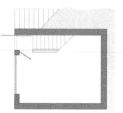

GARAGE

SECOND FLOOR

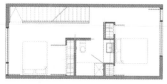

THIRD FLOOR

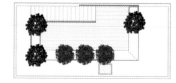

ROOFTOP

. . . .

ABOVE: The rooftop deck floats above Echo Park, offering a sweeping view from the coastal Santa Monica Mountains to the inland San Gabriel Mountains, with a glimpse of the Hollywood sign to cement its sense of place.

LEFT: Until recently, Simon ran his two-person architectural firm from the third floor. He delights in the 1920s apartment complex across the street, a bit of local history that was famously captured in iconic black-and-white photographs by renowned architectural photographer Julius Shulman.

ABOVE: Like each of the principal rooms in the house, the bedroom at the back of the third floor has a floor-to-ceiling window wall as wide as the room. Black wallpaper of Simon's design puts the focus on the window.

RIGHT: A galley kitchen with cabinets, fixtures, and appliances along one wall makes sense in this narrow space. A two-step change in floor level and a shift in floor surfaces define the cooking area from the eating area without walls getting in the way.

FAR RIGHT: A single well-placed skylight is a pleasant surprise—and a source of natural light—for the bathroom in the center of the third floor, the only bathroom in the house and the only space that doesn't benefit from a large window wall.

And, until recently, one of the two third-floor bedrooms served as Simon's architectural office!

Simon received special permission from the planning department to build right up to the lot lines, but the lack of setbacks meant that the house could not have windows on either side. To make up for it, Simon placed giant windows on the front and back ends of the house. The oversize windows bring light deep into the house and provide dramatic views. Alongside the windows in the living room and bedrooms is a solid-wood door that opens for air and light but provides a bit of privacy when closed. A metal railing spans the door openings for safety. In place of a big window in the kitchen, a pivoting glass door opens to a small backyard deck under a prolific avocado tree.

"From our perch on the corner," Simon says, "we see everything that happens, from drug deals to photo shoots." A lot of people come to this corner to take selfies and head shots. "They choose it," he thinks, "because it looks like they went somewhere." By which Simon means somewhere other than Los Angeles. But perhaps what they've discovered in the 1920s apartments and in Eel's Nest and the other hillside houses is a Los Angeles from a time gone by, one they perhaps never knew. ▌▌▌

"What attracted me was the view out the front window. The house is centered on the street, with an elevated view down the middle of it."

—Simon Storey, architect and homeowner

Placing a straight flight of stairs along one wall maximizes livable floor space in this 15-ft.-wide house. The open stairs and a see-through "wall" of thin studs allow space to flow and light to cascade down from the third floor.

architect
ADBC ARCHITECTURE

location
EMERYVILLE, CALIFORNIA

family compound

· · · ·

LEFT: Ben's sister lives at the back of the long lot in one of two houses that came with the property. The gate and pathway provide her with access to the street and welcome her home.

ABOVE: The orange door, concrete driveway pavers, and rusted steel gate hint at the modern kitchen at the rear of the house, but the house remains a classic bungalow, much to Ben and Adriana's delight.

t his is a story about a kitchen remodel in Emeryville, a small city wedged between Berkeley and Oakland. But it's also a story about much more than that. Realizing that they couldn't afford to buy a house independently, architects Ben Corotis and Adriana Daringa joined forces with Ben's sister, Lindsay, to look for property. They were hoping for just the right duplex. What they found instead was a long lot with two houses on it, an early-20th-century bungalow on the street and a 1950s house behind it. Lindsay wanted the back house; it had more privacy, and it was move-in ready. Ben and Adriana happily took the bungalow, which they were eager to fix up.

Ben and Adriana are modernists, but the bungalow form suits them. "Bungalows have the potential to be redone," Adriana says. "Rooms are offset just right, doorways shift, everything isn't lined up. So you can easily expand or reorganize space, add a half bath, fit in a closet." And yet bungalows typically follow a functional two-zone organizing principle: Public living spaces are on one side, private bedrooms and baths are on the other side. Ben and Adriana stayed within this pattern and simply expanded the kitchen into what had been a mudroom.

In remodeling the kitchen, they flexed their modernist muscles but respected the original house in scale. Bungalows are a decidedly domestic

115

house type; they're more about everyday family life, less about entertaining or making a grand impression. So it is with the new kitchen, which is crisp and streamlined but also warm and inviting. At 12 ft. by 21 ft., it's ample but not large. The lowered wood ceiling of the addition subtly divides the space into a cooking area and an eating area, enhancing its domestic scale. A double-sided fireplace connects the

"We have the doors open all the time. We didn't add square footage, but the house feels much bigger because the yard has become a part of our living space."

—Benjamin Corotis, architect and homeowner

. . . .

ABOVE: The thin ipe siding on the addition continues the lines of the narrow clapboards on the original house. The slats on the sliding screens were angled to block sunlight during summer and let in sunlight during winter.

LEFT: The remodeled kitchen opens to a backyard patio between Ben and Adriana's house and Ben's sister's house (not seen). Ben's sister has a deck on the far side of her house, but she often sits with Ben and Adriana on the patio and chats over a glass of beer or wine.

. . . .

TOP AND ABOVE: Birch plywood cabinets, stainless-steel countertops, and fiber-cement floor panels lend the kitchen a clean look. Built-in cabinets conceal a stacked washer/dryer. A Douglas fir ceiling defines an addition to the kitchen that replaced a leaky mudroom.

ABOVE RIGHT: Ben and Adriana gave up a window over the kitchen sink (which looked right at the neighbor's house, anyway) and opted for a tall window that defines a cozy nook and affords a peek at anyone coming through the sideyard gate.

kitchen to the original dining room. Where the old ice chest once stood are open shelves and a small nook, a few square feet of floor space that hold the key to the new-old quality of the kitchen.

In the country houses Adriana remembers from her childhood in Romania, not all rooms had fixed uses. Any room might have a small table in it that could transform into a dining table. One of her grandmothers lived in a kitchen building that was separate from the house. She slept in the kitchen, and Adriana and her family would sit on the bed, pull up a table, and have dinner there. It's something like that in the remodeled kitchen. When their daughter was very young, she and Adriana would sit on blankets in the nook and read books. Ben and Adriana have since put a little table in the kitchen so their daughter can draw while they cook. "If I had a choice," Adriana says, "I'd probably have a bed in the kitchen, right next to the fireplace. It's the place where the cat wants to be." ▥

architect
OFFICE OF ARCHITECTURE

location
BROOKLYN, NEW YORK

70/30 row house

A one-story addition at the back of the row house was replaced with two stories—a master bedroom above and a multipurpose living space below—both open to the backyard.

after Rachel and Zach bought their row house in Brooklyn, they went through an exercise that their architect, Aniket Shahane, highly recommends to his clients: Consider the least intrusive design solution—in terms of time, disruption, and cost—as well as the maximum effort. "Even if you can't afford the maximum scheme," Aniket says, "at least you know what you're giving up." In the end, Rachel and Zach opted for the more involved scheme—shoring up the rickety house and creating a 1,121-sq.-ft., two-bedroom, two-bath unit for themselves and an income-producing 500-sq.-ft., one-bedroom, one-bath rental unit, a 70/30 split. Their stipulation to Aniket was that, should they decide down the road that they wanted to occupy the entire building, they would not have to go through six months of construction.

The trick for Aniket was where to place stairs, plumbing, and electrical service and how to arrange the bathrooms to make it as easy as possible to convert the building from two units to one. Despite the slim, 15-ft. width of the building, Aniket found a way to fit in two staircases—a straight run leading from the front entry to the second-floor rental unit, and a compact, three-quarter turn staircase from the living area of the main unit to the master suite upstairs. The rental unit is separated from the master suite by a 3-ft. length of wall at the center of the building. To occupy the entire second floor, Rachel and Zach would simply have to remove the wall and an IKEA cabinet in the rental unit, then remove the rental unit's small IKEA kitchen.

LEFT: The existing addition was substandard, built without a foundation, right on the ground, so it made sense to replace it.

BELOW: In deciding to include a rental unit in their Brooklyn row house, Rachel and Zach calculated the optimal size of the unit and the amenities it needed to attract tenants, in order to contribute to their mortgage without taking away too much space from their own unit.

> *"There's a little wall on the second floor that separates the tenant unit from the master suite. Behind that wall is an IKEA cabinet. That's the only thing keeping them from expanding and taking over the whole floor."*
>
> —Aniket Shahane, architect

There's enough room on the first floor for a bedroom and bath and a multi-purpose space that serves as kitchen, dining room, and living room. The cooking area is actually quite large; it even has two sinks, one along the wall next to the stairs and one on the peninsula. The sitting area, by contrast, is rather small; but, as Aniket puts it, "the whole space is all one hangout area." And it all opens to the backyard.

The row house is located in South Slope, near better-known Park Slope, with its stately brownstones. The row houses in South Slope tend to be more humble,

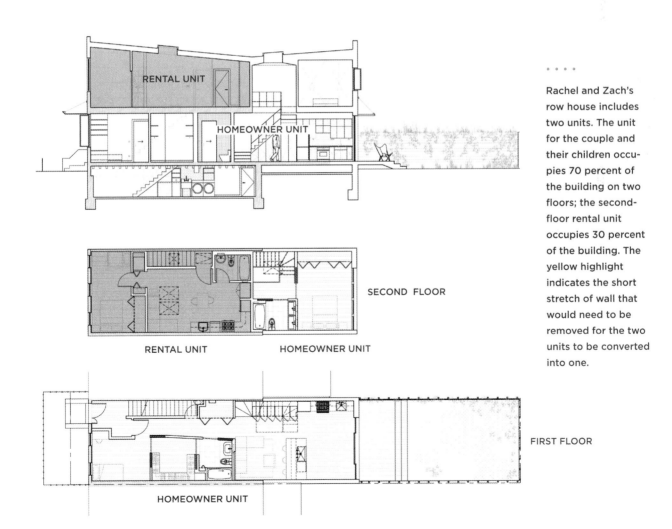

RENTAL UNIT

HOMEOWNER UNIT

SECOND FLOOR

RENTAL UNIT   HOMEOWNER UNIT

HOMEOWNER UNIT

FIRST FLOOR

Rachel and Zach's row house includes two units. The unit for the couple and their children occupies 70 percent of the building on two floors; the second-floor rental unit occupies 30 percent of the building. The yellow highlight indicates the short stretch of wall that would need to be removed for the two units to be converted into one.

For this remodel on a real-world budget, all of the kitchen cabinetry is from IKEA, spruced up with quartzite countertops (on which Rachel and Zach got a good deal) and drawer fronts from an outfit specializing in customizing IKEA cabinets.

faced in brick, wood, or, in the case of Rachel and Zach's house, vinyl siding, which they simply painted gray. Yet real estate is pricey in South Slope, as it is everywhere in the city, so it makes economic sense to build flexibility into a house, as Rachel and Zach have done. They're considering giving up the rental income, punching through the wall, and incorporating the rental unit into their home. Even if they do, then someday, perhaps as empty nesters, they could put the wall back and rent out the small unit again . . . or even move into the small unit and rent out the main one. It's nice to have options. ▮▮▮

LEFT AND FACING PAGE: The staircase in the owner's unit has several functions in addition to providing access to the master suite. Cabinets under the stairs serve as a pantry; the dark-stained oak stairs are a sculptural element in the quiet interior; and a skylight above the stairs sends natural light deep into the living space on the first floor.

architect
**ROBERT EDSON SWAIN
ARCHITECTURE + DESIGN**

location
SEATTLE

urban cabin revisited

· · · ·

What appears as a
cabin in the woods
is in essence the
same house that
stood on the barren
lot years ago (see
the top photos on
p. 126). Even the
deck is in the same
place, though now
there's a basement
ADU under it.

When Seattle architect Robert Edson Swain mentions
the need for refuge in a small house, he's talking about the way
he's configured his little city house so that it's possible to be
by yourself when others are there, or for several people to be doing different
things (perhaps listening to different music) at the same time. But he could
be talking about his need for refuge within the city. It isn't that he doesn't
embrace urban life. He works in Seattle, takes long walks through it, visits
friends all around the city. It's simply that he likes a respite in his own home.

In 1998, Bob purchased an utterly unremarkable house of 720 sq. ft. with
a small detached studio in Seattle's Phinney neighborhood. It's a delightful
neighborhood, with steep streets and jaw-dropping views west to the Olympic Mountains. But the house (built in 1905 as a worker's cottage) just stood
there in the middle of the lot, exposed. It didn't appear to offer the promise of
refuge, either within its walls or within the city.

Some 20 years later, the lot is a forested idyll, and the house has become
what Bob calls an urban cabin. For refuge from the outside, Bob intensively
gardened every inch of the lot, mostly with plants native to the Pacific Northwest. The urban cabin is really two cabins, and herein lies the secret to its
ability to provide refuge. Bob refashioned the studio into a bedroom, bath, and
study—his "back cabin." Within the original house—now his "front cabin"—he

125

Bob's urban cabin remodel began as an utterly unre-markable house, so lacking in distinction you couldn't even call it a bungalow. A third of the front yard was driveway.

fit in a living room with a small dining table, a galley kitchen, and a bedroom-and-bath suite. The cabins are separate structures in a kind of yin-yang relationship to each other, connected by a covered boardwalk. For many years, Bob had a house-mate, and, thanks to the twin cabin arrangement, both were able to find refuge when they wanted it.

Bob's house appeared in my 2006 book, *The Barefoot Home*, in which I wrote about its informality and indoor-outdoor connections, but that's not why this chapter is titled "Urban Cabin Revisited." It's so titled because Bob, in effect, revisited the house a few years ago when he excavated the crawl space and the area under the front deck to make room for an exquisite basement ADU. Taking

. . . .

ABOVE: Bob never tires of waking up in the back cabin, stepping outside, and taking in some fresh air as he walks a few paces to the front cabin for breakfast. By way of the boardwalk and a path of stepping stones, the garden flows between the twin cabins to a side yard with an ancient Chinese stone soak tub.

LEFT: The ultimate place of refuge is the bedroom in the back cabin, with a floor raised several steps above a low storage area. Bob is not looking at the skylights from the bed—he's in them. When he takes leave of houseguests to repair here, he's claiming his personal space, but he's also leaving them with the entire front cabin and ADU to themselves.

. . . .

ABOVE: You can use the furniture to scale the living room; it's just 12 ft. wide, the width of three sofas. It feels larger because your eye follows the rhythm of the purlins, collar ties, and rafters out to the deck and beyond to the garden.

RIGHT: The walk-out basement ADU is warm and snug, but it doesn't feel dark or cramped. A tall window opens to a narrow but gardened side yard. A mirror (behind the chair to the left) reflects the front of the room. Translucent panels that enclose the bathroom glow like a floor-to-ceiling lantern.

advantage of the steep slope on the west side of the lot, the ADU has ample windows and its own door to the side yard. A bookcase in the living room swings open to reveal spiral stairs down to the ADU.

Bob uses the ADU as guest quarters, or for dinners for up to a dozen guests, or to take in a film on a large projection screen. With the ADU, the house is still under 1,800 sq. ft., but now Bob has more places of refuge, as well as some options going forward. He might rent the ADU for extra income. Or he might rent the twin cabins. He owns some land on the Olympic Peninsula and plans to build a house there. Perhaps he'll retire to the country, he says, and keep the ADU as a pied-à-terre. That would make for plenty of revisits. ▋▋▋

• • • •

ABOVE LEFT: Architect Bob Swain is like a chess master, thinking several moves ahead. The initial remodel included the hidden-door bookcase that opened to a small storage space.

ABOVE CENTER: When Bob excavated the crawl space to add a basement ADU under the living room, the bookcase found its full expression as a door to stairs leading to the ADU.

ABOVE RIGHT: At the foot of the stairs is a passageway to the basement ADU that serves as a wet bar or a complete mini-kitchen, with a small refrigerator, a pull-out dishwasher, and a pull-out electric cooktop.

"Refuge is an essential element of survival in a small house."

—Bob Swain, architect

designer
FUNN ROBERTS

location
HOLLYWOOD, CALIFORNIA

one-room house

LEFT: A zigzag of translucent panels creates privacy from the street for those walking between the house (left) and converted garage spa (right). The outdoor panels echo the shoji-style panels inside the house.

ABOVE: The house appears as unassuming as it was when built as a carriage house in 1912, but a perforated steel fence and metal front door suggest inspired changes within.

the transformation of this little house in the heart of Hollywood began with a fence repair. The 603-sq.-ft. house was the home of a young actor when Funn Roberts—designer, builder, craftsman, artist—arrived to do some work on the fence. Custom outdoor furniture followed, and eventually the actor asked Funn to help him reimagine the house and a detached garage that stood near it. Almost 100 years earlier, in 1912, the house had been built as a carriage house for land baron Cornelius Cole, who owned a large swath of what would become Hollywood. Along the street in front of the house are three old ficus trees so enormous they form a kind of green sky over the sidewalk and yard. The one-bedroom house had some history to it, but the previous remodel had been uninspired, a mishmash of tiny rooms.

Funn crafted a new front door from steel and clad the fence with perforated steel, establishing an industrial modern look that felt just right to the actor. From there, Funn and the actor began a fruitful collaboration. "He would come with ideas, and I would come with ideas," Funn says, "and then I would figure out how to implement them." They took

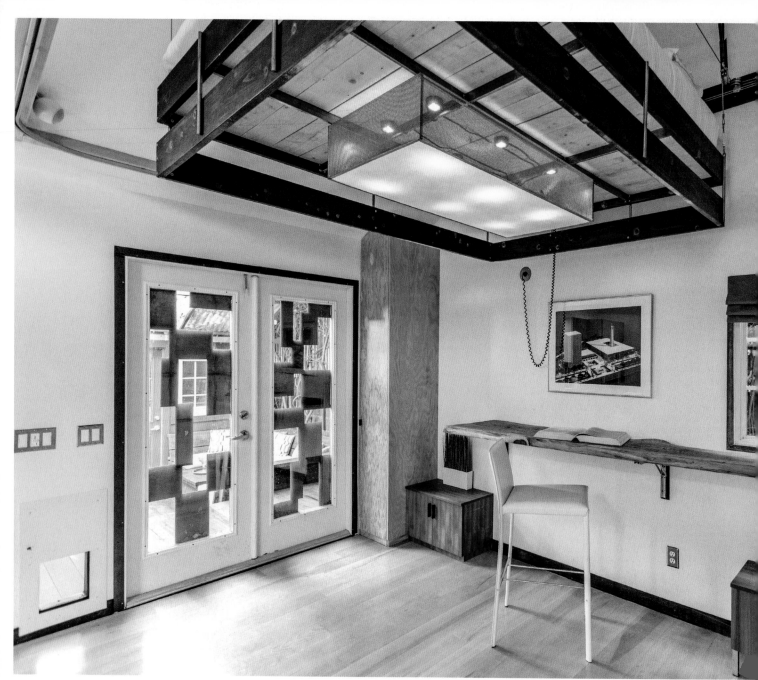

· · · ·

ABOVE AND RIGHT: Designer Funn Roberts dispensed with the notion of a Murphy wall bed and instead created a bed that descends from the ceiling. A live-edge desktop folds down to become the headboard. The owner liked to sleep by day. "You're an actor," Funn said to him, "let's surround the bed with a heavy stage curtain." When not in use, the curtain disappears into a small corner closet.

. . . .

LEFT: Behind shoji sliding screens, a walk-in closet and bath facilities are aligned in a narrow, boxlike enclosure within the house's one big room. The immediacy of the bath to the living space isn't for everyone, but packing storage and the bath into a narrow bar is key to creating a feeling of spaciousness in this 603-sq.-ft. house.

. . . .

ABOVE RIGHT: Translucent panels set in steel frames slide open to reveal a serene bathing space, with a sunken shower area and Japanese-style soaking tub. The sink is carved from a rock found in nearby Topanga Canyon —a hint of the wild that lingers just beyond the city.

down walls and opened up the ceiling, and Funn hit on the idea of running a screened bath enclosure along one side of the otherwise open space, transforming what had been a house with small rooms into one big room that feels like an urban loft.

As Funn and the actor continued to work together over several years, the house and garage evolved into an indoor-outdoor compound, with every square foot of the fenced lot contributing something to the experience. Everything Funn devised is a clever solution to a utilitarian need or an expression of exuberance, or both. The house is an exhibit hall of artful ideas for small-scale city living, ideas that would work equally well in a loft or a

> *"We made it a one-room shack
> instead of a one-bedroom house."*
>
> —Funn Roberts, designer

· · · ·

Just because a house and yard are small doesn't mean you can't have fun with them. The sitting area under a curved translucent roof becomes a magical oasis at night. There's a higher purpose to the roof; it keeps the thousands of berries that fall from the street's giant ficus trees from besmirching the deck.

studio apartment. Exhibit A is the bed, which can be hoisted to the ceiling, where it serves as a glowing light fixture and frees up the floor space beneath it.

Funn calls the place a shack, and it does have some of the laid-back qualities of a California surf shack. But this is Hollywood. Not only is it not a shack, but it's not even just one room, in the sense that the house is connected by a covered deck to the garage, which has been turned into a spa. The spa has two rooms—steam room and dry sauna—as well as a powder room, twin showers, and a laundry area. In La La Land, this is what's known as having your priorities straight. III

live/work stable

. . . .

ABOVE: The original garage bay allows access to the architectural office on the ground floor and to the residence on the second floor. The double entry creates a pocket of space that acts as a buffer to the alley.

after several years of house hunting, architect Mark Lawrence and his wife, Cary, found a two-story brick building on a brick-paved alley in the historic Shaw neighborhood of Washington, D.C., within walking distance of Cary's workplace. In the 19th century, the building had been a horse stable, and local lore has it that the opening between the floors was used for pitching hay down to the horses. There was a bathroom on the first floor; otherwise, each floor consisted of 1,250 sq. ft. of open space. The plan was to turn the ground floor into an office for EL Studio, the firm Mark runs with architect Elizabeth Emerson, and to turn the second floor into a home for Mark and Cary.

Thanks to EL Studio's inspired design, the former stable is now an exemplary model of a timeless paradigm: a small city building with a work space on the ground floor and a living space above it. The building's alley-facing garage bay, wide enough for carriages to pass through, has become a clever double entrance for both the residence and the office. Moving past a rolling gate, you arrive in a transition space from which you have a decision to make. Continue straight

The staircase to the second-floor residence juts into the ground-floor office and is clad in translucent panels, creating a subtle connection between living and working spaces, upstairs and downstairs.

ahead, through folding glass doors, to the architectural office, or turn left and enter a side hall on your way to the second-floor residence, now home to Mark, Cary, and their two children.

To reach the residence, you climb stairs that rise from the side hall through the original floor opening. The second floor is organized around a central core that contains three closets, a laundry nook, a powder room, and a full bath. An open kitchen extends from the core into a living and dining space at the front of the building. You pass to either side of the core to reach the master bedroom and a second, small bedroom at the back. Because the core does not touch the exterior walls, you experience the full width of the building from each of the main spaces.

Space flows around a central core, making the house feel larger than its square footage. A notch in the corner above the stairs lets light from the skylight reach the powder room. Likewise, a translucent panel allows light from the master bedroom to reach the master bath.

ABOVE: The interplay of old and new is captured in this small detail, an opening in the overlaid drywall that reveals the original brick wall and a hitching ring for the horses stabled in the building long ago.

RIGHT: A ribbonlike, orange pipe railing accentuates the upstairs-downstairs connection. It took an artful metalworker collaborating with the design team and piecing together and shaping piping on-site to create the continuous railing.

"There's activity on the weekend with people living here, and there's activity during the week because of commercial use. It makes this place thrive all the time."

—Mark Lawrence, architect and homeowner

. . . .

ABOVE: The high walls of adjacent buildings create a courtyard behind the live/work building, a quiet refuge for the staff of the ground-floor architectural office or for the family members who live upstairs.

LEFT: Although the master bath occupies a space within a core at the center of the building, it opens to the well-lit master bedroom and draws more natural light from a translucent panel above the tub.

During the week, the alley below is animated by businesses that open onto it and by frequent visits from service vehicles. On the weekends, Mark and Cary put up cones to create a safe space in which their children and neighboring children can play. The grown-ups will gather in the evening for impromptu meetings or to share a glass of wine while the children scoot around between the cones. III

designer
MARK EGERSTROM DESIGN

location
WEST HOLLYWOOD,
CALIFORNIA

bungalow opens up

. . . .

LEFT: The cedar-clad addition announcing the front entry takes its shape from the staircase to the roof deck. Putting the stairs outside, cantilevered from the building, kept them from taking away precious space from the loft inside.

ABOVE: The slimmest of outdoor spaces offers a moment of respite between the glass corner of the new living room and the original cottage, clad in ebonized cedar to match the addition. The door leads to a back bedroom now outfitted as an art studio.

Not many people can say that their house is a few blocks from Johnny Depp's notorious nightclub, the Viper Room. Interior designer Mark Egerstrom can say that about the 1,200-sq.-ft. house in West Hollywood he shares with his partner, Brian, and their young son. The house began life in the 1920s as a 600-sq.-ft. worker's cottage, built by Moses H. Sherman, who launched the Pasadena and Pacific interurban electric railway and gave his name to the town that would become West Hollywood. Mark's house is one of a handful of these cottages remaining in their original cluster. His house faces the street, but the others are reached through a pedestrian alley. Everything else around the little houses has been built up, though there's still a school less than a mile away that Sherman built for his workers.

Some of the cottages have their vintage detailing and charm intact, but the cottage Mark bought had its character stripped away through neglect and a series of shoddy remodels. Renovation was a given. Mark also wanted to add space, but in a way that would complement the original cottage and not overwhelm the neighboring cottages.

RIGHT: Glass walls don't put a hard stop to the interior. The fence and hedges at the edge of the small lot are the true walls of the living room. Sheets of glass were fused at the factory to create the corner sections, which were delivered and installed fully formed.

BELOW: Frameless glass serves as a partition between the shower and the rest of the bathroom, and as the exterior door to an enclosed outdoor shower. This being a small house with minimal yard space, the outdoor shower doubles as a dog-washing location.

. . . .

BELOW LEFT AND RIGHT: In the kitchen, spatial continuity is achieved through details like a frameless shower glass wall and floating corner cabinets that let the floor pass under them. Your eye travels beyond the shower glass to the cedar siding of the cottage, as well as through the opening over the sink, beyond the glass at the far end of the living room, to a fence clad in the same cedar boards as the cottage. You feel a sense of spaciousness although you're in a very small kitchen.

The lot is so small that Mark couldn't build out, so he built up, fitting a modern addition between the cottage and the pedestrian alley. The addition is just 15 ft. by 25 ft., but it's 20 ft. high, tall enough for a loft studio overlooking an otherwise modestly sized living room that soars the full height. On top is a generous roof deck that replaces the outdoor space taken up by the addition. "Our yard is up on the roof," Mark says. Within the original footprint, Mark turned the living room into a kitchen that connects to the new entry area and living room. The old kitchen became the master bedroom. Somehow Mark managed to squeeze in a staircase to the loft, with a powder room under it.

The addition is a master class in the continuity of space and materials and a testament to the value of paying scrupulous attention to even the smallest details. Mark quotes fashion editor Diana Vreeland,

> *"With a new house, it's you creating the story; with a remodel, you don't fully know what you're going to get. I almost like remodels more in that way. You're allowing the house to speak."*
>
> —Mark Egerstrom, designer and homeowner

• • • •

Especially in fair-weather cities like Los Angeles, there's nothing like a roof deck to add outdoor living space to a little house. Mark's deck looks south to the Pacific Design Center, designed by architect César Pelli.

who famously said, "The eye has to travel." It's a notion Mark applies to interior design. You can see it—and feel it—from the kitchen, glancing between tall cabinets. Your eye travels through a short hallway, through the bath (fixtures discreetly out of view), and through the shower glass to a fenced outdoor shower area. The horizontal fence boards slip past your framed view. You can't help but wonder: What might be beyond the frame?

If you could see around the corner, beyond the hedges surrounding the yard, then what you might see would be Mark and Brian walking their son to the elementary school Moses H. Sherman built. In a very real way, they're living out the vision Sherman had for this neighborhood all those years ago. ▮▮▮

architect
DAVID EISEN

builder
MORSE CONSTRUCTIONS

location
CAMBRIDGE, MASSACHUSETTS

colorful colonial

· · · ·

On the outside,
the house remains
essentially the
same colonial it
was in 1886. It's
on the remodeled
inside that it opens
up and becomes
lighter and brighter,
like a geode.

builder Paul Morse worked closely with architect David Eisen to remodel a 1,300-sq.-ft. colonial for Anna and Jim, their two young daughters, and an au pair. The house was built in 1886 in a densely packed neighborhood of Cambridge, across the Charles River from Boston. It's a narrow house, just 18 ft. 4 in. by 30 ft. 6 in., and it stands on a lot that's a mere 44 ft. by 50 ft. The floor plan couldn't be more basic: in essence, stairs at the center with a room to either side on each of two floors and an attic floor. With a few smart design moves and careful attention to detail, Paul and David found a way to open up the house, add natural light, and make the small rooms work better for the family.

A few of the changes seem almost like sleight of hand. Eliminating a closet and an exterior door at the back of the kitchen created room for an efficient "L" of kitchen counters (something the previous kitchen lacked); shifting the cabinets toward the back freed up space for French doors leading to a small outdoor eating area, itself made possible by removing bulkhead stairs to the basement. Changes like these might best be described as rejiggering, which the dictionary defines as "to rearrange in a new or different way."

145

> *"I tell my carpenters, 'Pay attention to every quarter inch on the first floor, because when you get upstairs it's going to matter.'"*
>
> —Paul Morse, builder

. . . .

ABOVE: Built-in cabinetry in the master bedroom takes up less space than closets. The recessed window seat feels like added space.

FACING PAGE: Open shelves between the stairway and kitchen help both spaces feel less confined. Playful colors have transformed the still modest kitchen. The glass-fronted cabinets and the open shelves let you sense the full depth of the space.

A great example of rejiggering is the reconfiguration of the second floor. The original bathroom (the only one in the house) occupied a space between the bedrooms. The stairs brought you to a landing at the back of the house; a long hallway then brought you to the bathroom at the front. Paul and David eliminated the back-to-front hallway and found space for two full bathrooms at the back, one to either side of the stair landing. The master bedroom expanded into what had been the hallway. The former bathroom space became a small office. Chinese puzzle solved!

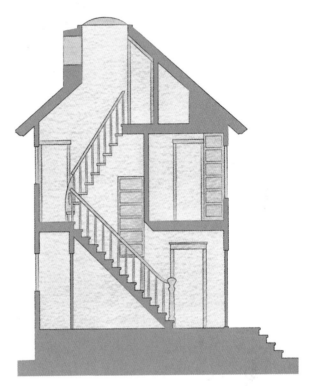

• • • •

Natural light from a 6-ft. by 6-ft. skylight spills down two flights of stairs at the center of the house. Transom windows over the doors allow the light to reach the bedrooms. An interior leaded-glass window brings light into a small upstairs office. The curved boards at the base of the steep attic stairs support the railings without the bulk of a traditional newel post.

In this house of three small floors, moving up and down the stairs is a big part of the daily experience. Instead of denying this, the remodel celebrates it. The main stairs now climb past open shelves with a peekaboo view into the kitchen, and the steep stairs to the au pair's attic rooms have become a sculpture that delights every time you see it, a signature element. By popping a sizable 6-ft. by 6-ft. skylight into the roof, Paul and David turned what had been a dark stairway in the middle of the house into a light well that channels sunlight into every room.

Anna has an eye for color, a nod to her Scandinavian heritage, and she deftly introduced bold colors throughout. Along with abundant natural light, the bright colors offer a fresh take on life in a colonial house without denying the domestic scale and spirit of the original. ▮

architect
TODD DAVIS ARCHITECTURE

location
SAN FRANCISCO

industrial conversion

FACING PAGE: Cutting the middle of three concrete buildings in half created a pavilion within a courtyard. The root ball of a sugar gum tree that had to be removed is playfully suspended from the ceiling. Sunlight streams through holes that had pierced the concrete for vent pipes in the structure's former life. The courtyard provides outdoor living space, a touch of green, and a window to the sky—none of which is easy to come by in a highly urban setting.

ABOVE: Architect Todd Davis sees the garage as a cedar and concrete sculpture, something artful to give back to the neighborhood. A street-facing garage is unusual, but it fits the local mix of houses and warehouse buildings.

Serendipity might be the best way to explain how this 1,215-sq.-ft. house in San Francisco's Mission District came about. Elliot purchased a most unusual place to call home, a dilapidated former industrial lot with three concrete buildings on it. He and his girlfriend, Kiyoko, decided to get married there, but only after it was renovated. This was quite a challenge, but they had the good fortune to team up with architect Todd Davis. Todd sees potential where others see none, and he embraces genuine collaboration with his clients. Elliot likes to sketch ideas and is willing to roll up his sleeves and get stuff built. Todd has a passion for concrete and simple forms. It was an inspired match.

The compound had been a World War II munitions depot, later a laundry, and finally a design studio and bare bones residence of sorts. The placement of the three structures on the lot inverts the typical order of things. A concrete garage fronts the street. Another concrete structure sits in the middle of the lot. The living spaces occupy a third building at the back of the lot. The back

ABOVE: The functional, off-the-shelf kitchen is evidence that you can do a lot with a little. The windows and skylights were existing. The cabinetry is custom, but Elliot shopped for tile seconds and laid out the pattern himself.

"Most people want the traditional, they don't want to take a risk. Or they can't see it. Elliot was, like, 'Oh, yeah, that's what I want!'"

—Todd Davis, architect

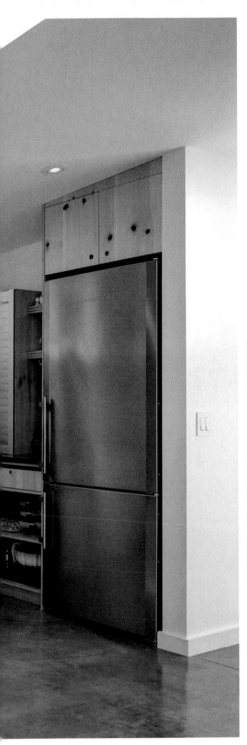

ELEVATIONS

FLOOR PLAN

· · · ·

ABOVE RIGHT: In the calm, inward-oriented living room, soft light falls from original steel sash windows with translucent glass. A green carpet echoes the grass in the courtyard.

building is a nonconforming structure; as a former legal residence that no longer meets zoning requirements, it can remain living space as long as it isn't torn down or expanded. Todd saw this as an opportunity to work with what was there.

Elliot and Kiyoko agreed with Todd's plan to leave the garage essentially as it was and to renovate the interior of the back building. They consider this Phase 1. The crux of the back-and-forth design process was what to do with the middle building. Todd's ingenious solution was literally to chop the middle building in half, creating an open dining pavilion within a courtyard, thus providing Elliot and Kiyoko with the outdoor space Kiyoko especially wanted.

ABOVE: The concrete pavilion, used for dining and art projects, offers a view to the residential structure at the back of the lot. French doors open to the master bedroom. With the security provided by the walled courtyard, the doors can stay open at night.

LEFT: A walkway from the street-side garage and front entrance passes the pavilion on its way to the residence. Moving through the courtyard, you experience the texture and qualities of knotty cedar, concrete, and galvanized metal. The simple but consistent palette of materials defines this as a unique place, set within—but also set apart from—the bustling city.

Elliot and Kiyoko love the natural light that streams into every room in their house from skylights or high-mounted windows. "The place is lit almost like a gallery," Elliot says. The high windows, some of which have translucent glass, don't afford big views, but because the house sits at the back of the lot, in line with a long stretch of neighboring backyards, there's a sense of space beyond the kitchen and living-room windows. The interior view from the master bedroom into the courtyard is magical.

Since the birth of their first child, Elliot and Kiyoko have begun imagining Phase 2, adding sleeping quarters above the garage. Elliot looks forward to moving beyond interior remodeling to building something completely new, clearly relishing another opportunity to help shape his family's home in the city. ▌▌▌

architect
A+I (ARCHITECTURE PLUS
INFORMATION)

location
NEW YORK CITY

found home

. . . .

LEFT: The former superintendent's unit included use of the alley behind the building. Brad and Susan created a walled garden connected to their unit by a roomlike, trellised deck. (The ramp beside the stairs is for their miniature dachshund.)

Unless you're in the market for a staggeringly expensive penthouse, here are some things you would not expect to find in a residence half a block from Central Park on New York's Upper West Side: "Green Roof Lawn," "Upper Deck," "Lower Deck," "Dog Ramp," "Fountain," '"Bamboo Grove," and "Garden Walk." Yet each of these is a label on architect Brad Zizmor's floor plan for the modest Upper West Side home he shares with his wife, Susan, a fashion executive, and their young son. It's not the result of having spent vast sums of money. Rather, it's the result of a rare find combined with design vision on the part of Brad and his architectural partner, Dag Folger.

The find was a 912-sq.-ft. former superintendent's unit on the ground floor of a co-op building. Another couple might have passed over the unit as dark, cramped, and none the better for its spot at the back of the building, facing an empty alley. Brad and Susan saw just what they were looking for . . . at least in their mind's eye. Granted permission to occupy the alley and alter the south-facing facade of the building, they realized they could create a strong indoor-outdoor connection and—counting the alley—double the size of their living space.

157

. . . .

ABOVE: Brad and Susan believe that the closer an outdoor space is to the level of indoor space, the more likely you are to use it. The deck takes full advantage of this principle. On the flip side, the garden 6 ft. below the deck gains a measure of privacy from the principle's inverse.

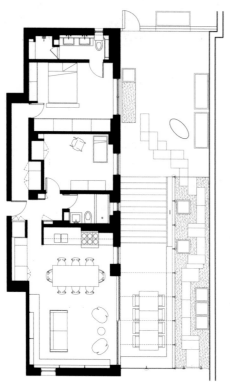

FLOOR PLAN

LEFT: On the north side of the unit is a narrow band of space that includes an entry area, a closet, and enough depth for a built-in refrigerator and cabinets. When Brad and Susan expanded their home into a small unit on the floor above, the hallway provided room for a staircase.

BELOW LEFT AND RIGHT: Because the co-op allowed changes to the facade of their ground-floor unit, Brad and Susan installed large windows in the master bedroom, overlooking their alley garden. The compact master bath maintains the boat-builder-like attention to detail seen throughout the house.

After an extensive remodel, the unit resembles neither a typical New York apartment, with its lack of a private yard, nor a townhome, with windows only at the narrow front and back ends, nor a penthouse, perched many stories in the air. "It's more akin to a rural home, or a home on a lake, a home built to address a particular view or landmark," Brad says. "Our landmark happens to be the garden." Indeed, every room in the unit orients to the garden through at least one window.

The living area opens through a wall of sliding glass onto a deck set 6 ft. above the garden, the highest terrain, as Brad puts it. The kitchen and dining areas connect to a series of less public spaces: bathroom, study, and master suite, each high enough above the garden to afford some privacy. A few years ago, Brad and Susan purchased the small unit above theirs and turned it into their son's place, accessed by its own staircase. It's the remotest space from the garden and the most private. "He has Greg Brady's attic," Brad says, in reference to the TV teen and his hip crash pad.

> *"We don't have a large, sweeping view or direct sunlight, but we have a little 'forest,' like you'd have at a place in the Berkshires or Adirondacks."*
>
> —Brad Zizmor, architect and homeowner

. . . .

ABOVE LEFT: Slats of ipe wood add warmth inside and out. By extending past the sliding glass doors, the slats visually connect the indoor living spaces and the deck. The gaps between the slats allow the walls to function as a shelving support system.

ABOVE RIGHT: As the garden extends from the deck, it becomes more private. At its far end, an opening planted with Shasta daisies offers a veiled peek into the alley beyond.

Including the upstairs addition, the combined unit is still a modest 1,500 sq. ft. It works because of the garden connection and storage fitted in everywhere (inspired by Dag's background with boats and Susan's desire to stay organized). In the midst of the densest city in America, here is a snug home with the feel of a cabin, the warmth of wood, and a garden just beyond. "We live in the city, yet we have a relationship with herbs, with gardening. . . ." Brad goes on to talk about the power of architecture to affect family life. His home makes a pretty convincing case. ▮▮▮

designer and builder
J.A.S. DESIGN BUILD

location
SEATTLE

sisters in the city

twin sisters Mary and Melinda lived in large suburban houses when they decided to pare down and find a small city house to share during their later years. They called on their close friends, Kim Clements and Joe Schneider, owners of J.A.S. Design Build. Kim and Joe pointed the sisters to a bungalow for sale across the street from the J.A.S. office, the perfect spot for a new life in the city, even though the house was a wreck. Mary and Melinda bought the house with confidence, trusting that J.A.S. could refashion it into a simple home for two sisters who, above all else, love to cook and enjoy good food with family and friends.

Kim and Joe run J.A.S. from a vintage brick storefront in Seattle's Wallingford neighborhood, a block from their own house. Wallingford is experiencing a boom in the construction of large apartment buildings, but it's still chock-full of Craftsman houses and bungalows, many with views south across Lake Union to downtown Seattle. Kim and Joe are passionate about sustaining the spirit of city neighborhoods like theirs, not by stopping growth—they're believers in urban density—but by

161

FACING PAGE: In this 1,069-sq.-ft. house for twin sisters who love to cook, the open kitchen occupies almost half of the living space. The kitchen is unencumbered by upper cabinets (there's a pantry beyond the narrow glass door) and is dominated by a generous, metal-topped chef's table that takes the place of a dining table.

thoughtfully updating and adapting existing houses and buildings, and by encouraging a balanced mix of building types, old and new.

Project architect Mike Freeman reconfigured the 1,069-sq.-ft. main floor as an open, multipurpose living space in front, with supporting rooms (two bedrooms, storage spaces, a bath, and a powder room) in back, separated from the living space by a thick wall of bookshelves. Given Mary and Melinda's culinary passion, it's no surprise that the main space is dominated by a hard-working kitchen. Instead of a dining table, the sisters opted for a huge chef's table, at which they serve guests and enjoy their everyday meals. The back rooms are small and delightfully spare. Between the two bedrooms is a walk-in closet with doors on either end, because Mary and Melinda wear each other's clothes!

Although the original house had its charms, in updating it and remaking it for the sisters, Mike chose to simplify it. A window bay was removed,

ABOVE LEFT: The main living space is open but ordered. A sofa and carpet establish a sitting area oriented to the woodstove. A thick wall of shelves divides the living space from the bedrooms and baths beyond. A drop-down desk stakes out a home office. The metal-topped chef's table marks the boundary of the kitchen and helps define a central pathway to the back rooms.

RIGHT: The beating heart of the house is an heirloom clock, handed down to the sisters from their father. Its special perch at the center of the house and the lack of distractions around it lend it a commanding yet calming presence.

The original house had fallen into disrepair. In an uncertain moment ahead of the remodel, Mary exclaimed, "I sold my house for this?"

> "In the city, your house is your block."
>
> —Kim Clements, creative director

the chimney and fireplace came down, and a small porch protruding from the front was replaced with a deep, full-width porch under the house's simplified roof form. Mike turned the walk-out basement into a rentable ADU that adds a housing unit to the neighborhood and can serve as quarters for a care provider down the road. The basement also includes a space for projects or storage that acts like a pressure-relief valve for the main floor. The remodeled house occupies the same footprint as the original, and it's still a bungalow, albeit with a pared-down aesthetic, as well suited to city living now as it was when it was built.

Kim and Joe believe that small houses often fail when they're forced to do too much. "It's like asking a pony to be a horse," Kim says. Mary and Melinda's house is not a scaled-down manor, it's a right-size city house. It has only so much storage; it has one big room that handles almost every aspect of living; it has bedrooms large enough for beds and not much else. It has one spectacular front window, not more; one magnificent working table in the kitchen, yet no dining table; a welcoming porch but no foyer. The house doesn't try to do everything; rather, it succeeds in doing a few things really well. ▐▐▐

. . . .

Two oversize wooden window sashes slide into wall recesses, creating an expansive opening that connects the main living space to the life of the street. Neighbors often sit on the porch or the wide windowsill for a chat with the sisters while they sit inside.

ADU
Accessory Dwelling Unit

the bike shed

. . . .

FACING PAGE: A number of design moves help the interior feel and function like a larger space: The space is tall, well lit, and open to the patio; the front door and patio doors swing out, not in; a window seat saves space around the dining table; and the kitchen neatly fits along a single wall.

ABOVE: In place of a garage that stored bikes, Sarah and Justin have a 650-sq.-ft. ADU that generates rental income when it's not occupied by family or friends. The ADU has a dedicated bike-storage room that makes up for the garage.

Sarah and Justin love their Northeast Portland neighborhood, with its free activities for kids, music and movies in a nearby park, and restaurants a few blocks north in the Alberta Arts District, known for its monthly street fair. They've made a mark on their own street, literally, with a mural they painted with neighbors, a project Sarah orchestrated. With the ADU they built behind their house, they're able to welcome family, friends, and Airbnb guests. Sarah and Justin are busy raising two young daughters, yet they've already given a passing thought to one day occupying the ADU as empty nesters. Perhaps this is one reason they built it to such high standards of durability and sustainability. The ADU is just 650 sq. ft., but it's rock-solid. As for energy use, it's close to net zero.

They found the perfect architect in Jack Barnes, who was willing to collaborate with them, eager to incorporate many of their ideas, and just as eager to contribute his deep knowledge of green design and building. Sarah and Justin call their ADU the "Bike Shed" because it replaced a garage in which they'd stored their bikes. Indeed, a key feature of the ADU is a dedicated bike-storage space with carriage doors that open to the driveway. The guest quarters include a multipurpose living area with

ABOVE AND RIGHT: The ADU takes full advantage of the corner lot. Both the ADU and the main house orient to the primary street. Guests reach the ADU by a path alongside the house. But the ADU's separate bike-storage room, used by the homeowners, opens to the cross street.

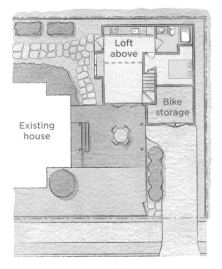

LEFT: The open interior showcases a spirited palette of materials and surface treatments: stained concrete floors, steel railings with panels of bike parts, steps painted by Sarah, and old boards salvaged from the garage that came down to make way for the ADU.

Loft above

Bike storage

Existing house

an efficient but fully functional kitchen, a bedroom, a bathroom, and a sleeping loft with a separate sitting area.

Jack managed to fit all of this into a tidy package that earned a Platinum Certification from Earth Advantage Institute for energy and resource efficiency, indoor air quality, and water conservation. The Bike Shed has the benefit of being small, but that's only a start. Jack gave it a simple shape that's easier to insulate and make airtight than a complex structure. He located windows for privacy and daylight but kept openings to a minimum to avoid heat loss. And he sloped the large, south-facing roof to best orient an array of photovoltaic solar panels. The panels supply almost enough power to meet the annual electricity needs of the ADU.

Jack also navigated the nuances of getting the proper permits for the ADU. Portland encourages secondary dwellings, but the city's building code must walk a fine line, balancing the needs of individual homeowners with the collective need

"In some ways, it's an ordinary exterior, but it's a house that's experienced more from the interior, so we tried to do something a little more dramatic inside that simple shell."

—Jack Barnes, architect

• • • •

Sarah and Justin express their fondness for bikes in a bicycle-part stair railing created by local artisan Alameda Metalworks, as well as in the street mural that they and their neighbors painted on their street, a popular bike route through Northeast Portland.

for street parking, open space, and buildings that fit the scale and spirit of a given neighborhood. Among the challenges are constraints on overall square footage and a requirement to visually relate the ADU to the main house in a number of ways. On top of that, the Bike Shed had to hold to a budget that Sarah and Justin calculated they could pay back with 10 years of rental income, and it had to be built to last. Jack appreciates that Sarah and Justin were willing to invest in "stuff that gets covered up"; that is, stuff you don't see, like insulation. What Sarah and Justin do see, more clearly than many, is how to shape a flexible future in the city without planning on having to move out. ▮▮▮

designer and builder
NEW AVENUE HOMES

location
BERKELEY, CALIFORNIA

susan's cottage

. . . .

What appears to be the front door to the cottage in fact opens to a much-needed storage shed. The shed is designed to look like an entry vestibule so that from the street the cottage reads as a little house. The entry door is around the corner to the left, facing the private backyard.

Susan loves her street in Berkeley, she's close with her neighbors, and she has a sister and good friends who live within walking distance. When she heard about a backyard cottage developed in Berkeley by New Avenue Homes, she thought about the cluttered one-car garage that stood kitty-corner to her house at end of her driveway. She had a vision of replacing the garage with a small storybook cottage, and she turned to Kevin Casey, founder of New Avenue Homes, to make it happen. New Avenue Homes is a national network of architects and contractors who use New Avenue's web-based software to manage the design and construction process. Kevin fondly recalls the many meetings that followed around the kitchen table at the back of Susan's house (where Susan hosts nonnegotiable weekly dinners for her sister and friends). From the same table, Susan now looks out at a diminutive cottage that enlivens her postage-stamp backyard.

Susan figures she can get value from the cottage in the near term by renting it through Airbnb or offering it to guests, but her ultimate plan is to move into the cottage herself and turn the main house over to her daughter, son-in-law, and grandchildren when they return to Berkeley from living and working overseas.

At 469 sq. ft., the cottage is small by most standards, but it has everything Susan imagines she'll need to live simply and efficiently: a

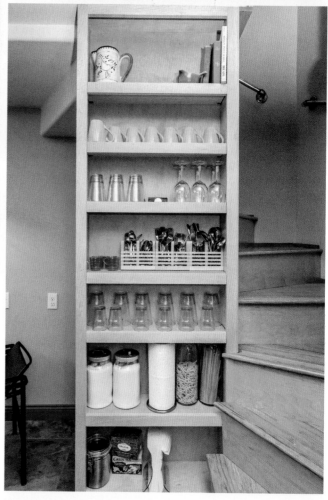

TOP AND ABOVE LEFT: Because the cottage sits perpendicular to the house, both look onto the same postage-stamp backyard without looking directly at each other.

BELOW: The cottage makes up for its lack of floor area with open space that flows up to the loft. The small size of the cottage allowed Susan to build with quality materials, even on her modest budget. Redwood from the garage that was taken down was reused for trim.

BELOW RIGHT: The loft is tall enough for the average person to stand up in. Stair access, closet space, and the ample ceiling height make the loft feel like a real room. The connection to the living space below and the skylights keep the space from feeling cramped.

multipurpose living space with a kitchenette, a full bath, several closets and storage areas, and a sleeping loft reached by stairs (not the quintessential ladder of many truly tiny houses). Take the same mini house and put it on two acres in the country or outer suburbs, and it might feel confining or isolating. But living in a house this small is a different story altogether when you're in the city, right beside extended family, close to neighbors, and near a lively downtown.

Until she moves into the cottage, Susan enjoys regular feedback through Airbnb confirming her decision to remain in the neighborhood she calls home. "We loved Susan's cottage in the heart of one of Berkeley's prettiest neighborhoods," commented one guest. "Close to shops and restaurants. Very walkable. Safe, quiet, and secluded." Many people build tiny houses on wheels to avoid being tied down. Susan built her little city house so she can stay put. ▐▐▐

LEFT: Susan's cottage has a tight staircase that turns 270 degrees around kitchen shelves (with a storage closet behind them). The three-quarter-turn stairs reach the middle of the loft, facing the same direction as the shelves.

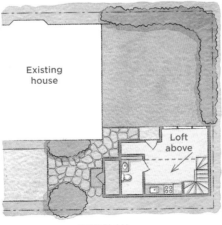

Existing house

Loft above

SITE PLAN

"Susan's backyard cottage is about flexibility, options, quality of life, and staying put."

—Kevin Casey, developer

designer and builder
ZENBOX DESIGN

location
PORTLAND, OREGON

garage ADU

- - - -

LEFT: Bryan regularly turns the quotidian into the unexpected. For the address on the garage ADU, he set screws partway into the siding to create raised numbers.

it happens all the time. Someone passing by mistakes Bryan and Jen's house for a new neighborhood watering hole. This is what comes of turning a garage on a corner lot in Portland into a hip home with a retracting wall of glass doors and an inviting patio.

Before moving into the garage of their three-bedroom ranch house, designer Bryan Danger and his wife and business partner, Jen Danger, first had to run away. They quit their jobs, rented out their house, and lived in a tricked-out Volkswagen bus for a few years while they drove south into Mexico and Central America. They returned for a pause in their travels, only to fall in love with Portland all over again. Rather than kick out their tenants (and give up the rental income), they rented an apartment down the street, and then realized they could move into their own garage.

To keep costs down—and because their van life had convinced them they needed very little to be happy—Bryan and Jen decided to create their ADU entirely within the existing confines of the 20-ft. by 24-ft. garage. The only walls they erected are for the bathroom, which, though enclosed at the back of the space, is well ventilated by an operable skylight. The space is heated by a natural-gas fireplace; a ductless, mini-split heat pump allows Bryan and Jen to offer AC when they rent out the ADU through Airbnb. The couple did almost all of the construction themselves. Their one splurge was for a folding glass wall system designed to fit within the existing garage-door opening.

"We design dream homes. They just happen to be under 800 sq. ft."

—Bryan Danger, designer

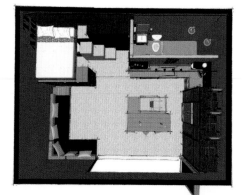

BELOW: Bryan and Jen's ADU is a converted garage at one end of an otherwise ordinary ranch house they own and rent out. They spend as much time on the terraced patio where their driveway used to be as they do inside.

BELOW RIGHT: Tucked behind the kitchen, the generous bathroom is washed in natural light and open enough for unfettered showers that feel like the outdoor showers Bryan and Jen take on their frequent van travels.

As friends, neighbors, and house-tour visitors experienced the garage ADU, they began asking Bryan for design help. Jen pointed out to Bryan that since he was up at all hours designing because he liked it, he might as well make it a business. He did, after all, have six years of architectural education. Bryan and Jen call their enterprise "zenbox design." Zenbox could be the name of their garage—as simple and pure a box as you'll find, turned into a small home with a few deft and delightful design moves.

ABOVE: The kitchen offers a lesson in using basic materials simply and honestly: concrete for countertops, oriented strand board for the floor, and reclaimed fir for cabinetry. A counter-on-wheels swings out to accommodate dining for four to six.

RIGHT: Pull-out steps are a clever way to reach a small loft. An earlier clever idea—designing the entire space around a rock climbing wall that was already in the garage—was nixed when Bryan and Jen realized the kitchen island would be right under the highest pitch!

Bryan and Jen realize that Portland is losing its bungalows at an alarming rate to teardowns that often result in much larger houses. There's no stopping growth in cities like Portland, but Bryan points out that ADUs add density without diminishing the stock of older houses. As far as Bryan and Jen are concerned, the smaller the ADU, the better. "Four-hundred and sixty square feet seems like plenty," Bryan says of their garage. "The last thing we'd do is build larger." He pauses and imagines if they had built their ADU from scratch. "We might have made it smaller," he says. ▌▌▌

designer
ZENBOX DESIGN

location
PORTLAND, OREGON

eco guest house

Pam and Justin thought about moving from their 700-sq.-ft. house in southeast Portland because they never had enough room for their frequent out-of-town guests, but they loved their backyard and the neighborhood too much to leave. Instead, they called designer Bryan Danger of zenbox design. They had toured the garage ADU Bryan shares with his wife and business partner, Jen Danger (see the previous chapter), and they asked Bryan to design a guest house. Pam and Justin wanted their ADU to have as many green features as they could afford, and they didn't want to give up too much of their backyard. As for look and feel, their simple 700-sq.-ft. house offered little in the way of inspiration; they wanted their ADU to have the aesthetic of Bryan and Jen's garage, which Pam describes as being "modern, with industrial touches, but also warm and livable."

Pam and Justin had Bryan and Jen over for a glass of wine, and Bryan began sketching ideas for what ultimately would become a 446-sq.-ft. guest house. It was going to be two stories, with a living roof and an array of solar panels. But small houses like ADUs are inherently expensive on a per-square-foot basis, and such features as a living roof and solar panels add expense up front. Bowing to budget realities, Pam and Justin opted to hold part of the house to one story and build just enough of a second story for the bedroom. They put the solar panels on their list of future improvements but kept

"One neighbor already had an ADU. After we started construction, we primarily got questions like, 'How can I do this, too?'"

—Pam, homeowner

NEAR RIGHT AND FAR RIGHT: There was room in the modest budget for a few flourishes, like floating steel and bamboo stairs with a tread that extends to become a desktop and a bookcase that serves as a railing.

LEFT: The two-story section of the ADU has a pitched roof and conventional lap siding, a nod to the style of homes in the neighborhood. The more modern single-story section to the back has natural wood siding and a living roof.

BELOW: The original design for the ADU included an awning of solar panels that shelters the south-facing patio doors. The initial budget could not absorb the cost of the panels, but Pam and Justin plan to install them in the future.

ABOVE: Several custom features help the first floor feel light and open, among them floating stairs, open kitchen shelves, and a countertop on wheels that serves the cook and then rolls away from the sink to seat six.

RIGHT: Really small kitchens look sharper with a cooktop unit set into the countertop above a separate oven unit built into the lower cabinet, an arrangement that avoids breaking up the flow of the countertop.

the living roof. Pam got a deal on 25 modular plant trays that were left over from a large green roof project in Seattle and installed them herself.

Renting the ADU through Airbnb was going to be a side gig, something to try for a weekend here and there. But the guest house has turned out to be a popular rental for people visiting the neighborhood, parents helping students move into college dorms, and people in town for weddings, funerals, and family reunions. Pam and Justin have found that they really enjoy being Airbnb hosts, even though it means sharing their backyard. One night, they started watching *Jurassic Park* on an outdoor projection screen. When their Airbnb guests returned, they offered to turn off the movie, but the guests said, no, since they, too, love *Jurassic Park*. And so the four sat down to a full screening over barbecue. ▌▌▌

shipping-container ADU

• • • •

ABOVE: Julio's backyard ADU is honest about what it's made of: two shipping containers in all their pale blue glory, complete with decals, light rust, and giant steel doors. By intention, the transformation from industrial box to home happens mostly inside.

One thing led to another would be the quickest way to explain how artist and designer Julio Garcia wound up with an ADU built from shipping containers in the backyard of a rental house he owned in Savannah, Georgia, about a mile from the historic downtown. But to tell the tale: Julio had a private painting studio on the corner of 38th and Price Streets that grew into a think tank for artists, designers, and architects and then morphed into a hands-on fabrication space. The collective, known as Price Street Projects, no longer had a clean, quiet space for thinking and designing, so Julio decided to build a small studio on property he owned. He'd been smitten by a shipping-container project he'd seen in Germany, and he was determined to build with containers as well.

As fate would have it, Savannah is a port with a ready supply of shipping containers, if you know who to ask. As Julio puts it, he knew somebody who knew somebody who knew somebody who worked at the port. Julio arranged to meet the gentleman from the port at Pinkie Masters bar (where Jimmy Carter announced his candidacy in 1976); several weeks later, Julio had two 40-ft.-long, 8-ft.-wide, 9-ft. 6-in.-tall containers and a set of drawings for turning them into an ADU.

Next came what Julio calls Phase Two: Delivery. A crane was too expensive, and airlifting the containers would have damaged the trees on the

By offsetting the shipping containers, Julio created two 8-ft.-wide nooks off the main space: one for an intimate sitting area (right), the other for a bedroom (above). The sweeping main space, by contrast, flows out to the leafy yard, especially when the container doors are swung open.

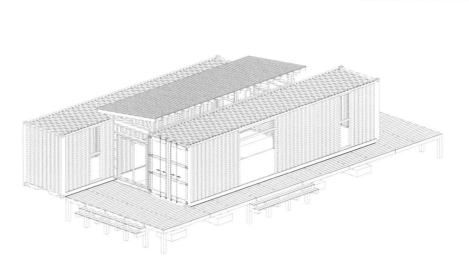

ABOVE RIGHT: The wood floorboards that define the kitchen area are original to the shipping container; plywood covers the rest of the floor. Steel beams connect the opened-up containers and carry the roof load. The corrugated roof of the containers (which are insulated above) quietly expresses the ADU's provenance.

property. The plan was to have a tractor trailer back the shipping containers deftly between the trees and onto a waiting foundation of concrete piers and steel beams. Julio went so far as to interview truck drivers until he found one with the right combination of skill and audacity. The process was supposed to take a few hours. It took all day. In the end, the containers were in place, offset and reversed, so that the doors at the ends of the containers would be on opposite sides of the ADU.

Julio's concept for making a proper building of the two shipping containers is as simple as it is brilliant. The containers stand 8 ft. apart. In between them is a site-built space that rises to 12 ft. and has clerestory windows that peek above the roofs of the containers. Each container has 27 ft. cut out of the side facing the in-between space,

> *"I tend to enjoy designs where the materials are themselves. . . . I like materials to be used in a natural way. If it's wood, let it be wood. If it's steel, leave it as steel."*
>
> —Julio Garcia, designer and homeowner

• • • •

To eliminate the narrow, cramped feeling of the inside of a shipping container, Julio cut 27 ft. of sidewall from two 40-ft.-long containers and added a tall, 8-ft.-wide section between them. The result is a bright, open space that feels nothing like a container.

thus creating a large, open space that feels like anything but a container. The clerestory windows and smartly placed patio doors flood the space with light and connect it to the wooded yard.

The shipping container ADU worked beautifully as a studio, but eventually Julio decided to relocate Price Street Projects, which is now based in Miami. Several months before leaving Savannah, he moved into the ADU with his family to experience living in it full-time. They loved it. "For me, it was all about seeing the project through," Julio says. ▐

designer
STEPHANIE DYER

location
PORTLAND, OREGON

compact backyard cottage

· · · ·

The two-story height of Stephanie and Sam's backyard cottage gives it presence well beyond its 342 sq. ft. But it's just 15 ft. by 18 ft., with one multifunction room downstairs and a sleeping loft and bathroom upstairs.

t he **342-sq.-ft. cottage** that interior designer Stephanie Dyer and her husband, Sam, built behind their one-bedroom bungalow in Portland's historic Mississippi district is, unmistakably, a companion to their house. The cottage is taller and smaller than the house, but it has the same narrow Dutch lap siding, painted the same deep brown with sunflower-yellow window sashes. The house and the cottage have matching stoops made from cement tiles of Stephanie's design. Both have benefited from Stephanie's creative talent and Sam's skill as a carpenter. Yet the story of the cottage is bigger than that of Stephanie and Sam. From its inception, the backyard cottage was a family affair, a labor of love that included both Stephanie's parents and Sam's parents.

With Stephanie and Sam's first child on the way, the four soon-to-be grandparents (going way beyond the minimum cordiality expected of in-laws) considered buying a condo together so they could make longer and more frequent visits. It was Sam's father who suggested replacing Sam and Stephanie's garage with an ADU. Stephanie assumed the role of lead designer, with her parents and in-laws working together as one client. Having designed and built his family's house back in Wisconsin, Sam's dad was an especially enthusiastic participant, doing research and pitching in with interior work. He was pleased, this time around, to defer to a general contractor.

189

The ADU has its own form, different from the house, but it has a compatible look, with the same Dutch lap siding as the house, the same yellow window trim, and the same tiled stoop.

The design of the cottage reflects Portland's zoning and ADU regulations combined with Stephanie's penchant for keeping things simple. The east wall of the cottage was required to be a windowless firewall. So it made sense to place the stairs along the east wall and to open up to the garden on the west side with a 2-ft.-deep bump-out and lots of windows. Stephanie placed the bathroom directly above the kitchen to keep the plumbing to one wall. Backed by research from Sam's dad, she determined that a small direct-vent gas fireplace could heat the whole cottage, without ductwork or complicated mechanical systems. By locating the fireplace in the two-story space just beyond the door, Stephanie ensured that heat would reach the sleeping loft, to be redistributed by a large ceiling fan. She and Sam spent time figuring out where exactly to place windows and operable skylights to generate cross-ventilation, so cooling is equally simple.

ABOVE: The breakfast nook takes advantage of a 2-ft. bump-out to provide the essence of a dining room, living room, and study—plus guest room, since the booth converts into a queen-size bed. After a meal, you can stretch out on the seats and read by the fireplace.

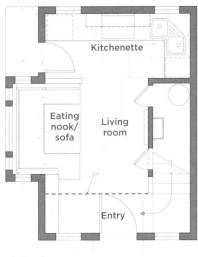

Kitchenette

Eating nook/sofa

Living room

Entry

FIRST FLOOR

Sleeping loft

Open to below

SECOND FLOOR

"The fun part of an ADU is that it's like a playhouse. But I also think they're so versatile."

—Stephanie Dyer, designer

. . . .

The staircase and fireplace surround feature patterned, ceramic tiles designed by Stephanie. Going up and down the wide stairs, you don't feel like you're in a mini-house. The gas fireplace provides a touch of home, plus all the heat the cottage needs.

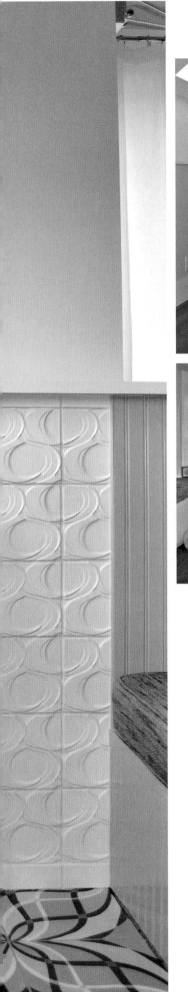

NEAR LEFT: Stephanie could have extended the second floor over the entry area to buy enough space for a private bedroom with a closet. But the sleeping loft allows the whole interior to feel like a unified volume. The 42-in.-high cabinet suffices as minimalist clothing storage.

BELOW LEFT: The corner windows and the side door to the garden create a feeling that space continues beyond the room itself. The flow is more than visual; opening the front and side doors along with windows on three sides generates wonderful cross-ventilation.

BELOW RIGHT: A queen-size bed takes advantage of the 2-ft. bump-out directly above the eating booth in the breakfast nook bump-out. Although someone has to climb over someone else when two are in the bed, both get to enjoy the feeling of sleeping in a treehouse.

On the one hand, they treated the ADU like a boat: fitting in storage under the booth seating, appointing a narrow cabinet in the sleeping loft for hanging clothes, sneaking a stacked washer/dryer into a closet off the bathroom. On the other hand, they built thick walls with wide window trim, embellished the interior with ceramic tiles of Stephanie's design, and constructed the stairs with thick wood treads. The result is a compact cottage with the solidity and comfort of a full-size house.

Sadly, Sam's father passed away before the ADU was finished. But the little cottage is there for Stephanie and Sam and their two children, their extended family, and guests fortunate enough to choose it as a short-term rental. Sam's mother now spends her winters in the cottage, far from Wisconsin. Stephanie recalls the many times she has found her mother-in-law sitting with her grandson in the breakfast nook, each occupying half of the booth. "There are probably a lot of Legos in those cushions," Stephanie says with a smile. III

three vancouver
laneway houses

o book of little city houses would be complete
without its share of laneway houses, the small, backyard ADUs
that are popping up throughout the Canadian city of Vancouver,
British Columbia. (In Vancouver, alleys are called laneways.) Vancouver's laneway houses are a response to the city's desire for greater density, a lack of vacant land, and the astonishingly high price of housing within the city. The

. . . .

LEFT: Contemporary Laneway House. This compact laneway house for a couple with a young child takes advantage of a corner lot across from a park.

CENTER: Laneway Classic. It's remarkable that two bedrooms and two baths fit within this 675-sq.-ft., story-and-a-half laneway house.

RIGHT: Live/Work Laneway House. Built on a family-owned lot, this spirited, 760-sq.-ft. laneway house for one includes a loft studio.

hope of many who can't afford to own or rent their own house is that they might be able to swing a little house in someone else's backyard.

So much the better if the backyard is already in the family. A significant number of laneway houses are being built by young adults on city lots owned by their parents, or by aging parents on lots owned by their adult children, or even in their own backyards. Often, building a laneway is the only affordable way for someone to return to the neighborhood in which they were raised, or to stay in the neighborhood where they've grown old.

Since 2009, the year Vancouver established bylaws allowing laneway housing, about 2,500 laneway houses have been built in the city. Along the way, designers and builders have honed strategies to address the sometimes arcane stipulations of Vancouver's laneway house regulations and turn potential constraints into opportunities. You'll see these strategies in each of the three laneway houses featured here.

designer and builder
LANEFAB DESIGN/BUILD

location
**VANCOUVER,
BRITISH COLUMBIA**

contemporary laneway house

· · · ·

FACING PAGE: The open living space has room for large furniture and a full-size kitchen. The master bedroom upstairs benefits from storage built into the space under the gabled roof.

ABOVE: The house is something of a hybrid, with a traditional gabled roof but modern detailing. Metal roofing, rock stucco walls, and cedar details are low key and low maintenance.

In most cities, the value of land plays an outsize role in the cost of owning a house. This can make even a little city house an absurdly expensive proposition. On the other hand, if the land is already owned by a family member and another family member builds a small second house on it, then the tables turn. Even at a high cost per square foot, the little house becomes a good deal. Such was the case for Bruce and Nicole, a young couple with a new baby. For less than half the cost of the 1,000-sq.-ft. condos they were contemplating, they were able to build a similar-size laneway house on property already owned by Bruce's parents, gaining the advantage of extended family next door, a little outdoor space, and a large city park across the street.

The couple hired Bryn Davidson and Mat Turner, founders of the design-build firm Lanefab. Bryn and Mat's laneway houses employ many green strategies, including Lanefab's signature extra-thick walls, which combine airtightness and several layers of insulation. "A home with thick walls is more comfortable, it's quieter, and it saves energy without relying on complicated technologies," Bryn says. He also likes the way a home with thick walls looks. "The deep window recesses add visual interest and make the building feel

"Most of our clients are in the process of starting their own families. A laneway house built on their parents' property is affordable, and they have the ability to swap homes with their parents when needs change."

—Bryn Davidson, founder, Lanefab

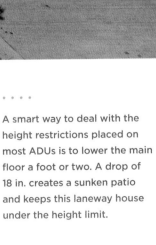

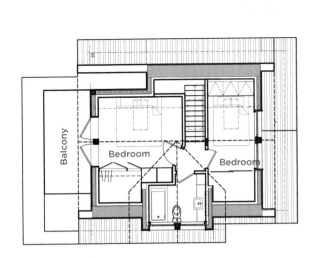

SECOND FLOOR

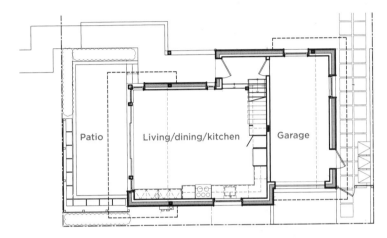

FIRST FLOOR

A smart way to deal with the height restrictions placed on most ADUs is to lower the main floor a foot or two. A drop of 18 in. creates a sunken patio and keeps this laneway house under the height limit.

. . . .

TOP: A built-in bench behind the dining table provides seating and storage. Its low profile and simple design reduce visual clutter.

ABOVE: A small raised area serves as both entry space and stair landing. The two steps down to the living space are subtracted from the straight run of stairs to the bedrooms, enabling the staircase to be shorter in length.

more substantive," Bryn says, "like the brick and stone buildings in many older cities." Thick walls could have presented a problem for laneway houses, given the limits set on square footage, but with Lanefab's encouragement, Vancouver adopted a policy, called a "thermal exclusion," that doesn't penalize extra wall thickness in calculating the area of a laneway house.

Bruce and Nicole's ADU replaced a garage on the corner of the street and the laneway, an ideal location. The 750-sq.-ft. house was built with its own attached 300-sq.-ft. garage, as required of laneway houses at the time, though garages are no longer mandatory. The first floor consists of a single open kitchen/dining/living space. Bruce and Nicole wanted a large living area, so they were willing to compromise on the size of the bedrooms under the gabled roof. The smaller of the two is just wide enough for a double bed. But the spaces are comfortable and bright, well lit by large windows and skylights. With bedrooms this snug and delightful, it seems like a good trade-off. ▌▌▌

designer and builder
SMALLWORKS

location
**VANCOUVER,
BRITISH COLUMBIA**

laneway classic

Jake Fry started his Vancouver-based firm, Smallworks, several years before the 2009 bylaws that allowed laneway houses in the city, first advocating for laneway housing, then becoming a practitioner. He initially drew inspiration for his laneway houses from the catalogs of the 1920s put out by Sears and others that offered basic, affordable houses as kits. What people expected from a house back then, Jake says, was much more modest than what's typically expected of a house today. Jake talks about the "grace and practicality" of the catalog houses. "We want to rediscover the simple elegance a home can have," Jake says, "and part of that is modest size."

A large percentage of laneway houses in Vancouver are being built by developers who tear down a house and replace it with a new house plus a laneway house, a two-for-one deal that adds square footage to the property and profit to the balance sheet. Jake made a decision early on to work only on laneway houses that were built behind an existing house. "We want to preserve the housing stock by adding housing to neighborhoods in a very subtle way," Jake says, "and keeping the principle residence is an important part of that." As a result, most of Smallworks's clients have a familial

RIGHT TOP: Although the house is quite traditional on the out-side, the interior features a clean-lined, contemporary kitchen and smooth, concrete floors.

RIGHT BOTTOM: The street-side entry area is flanked by a staircase and a small closet. The staircase creates a little separation between the kitchen and the living space (and hides the refrigerator).

Two bump-outs—a shed dormer and a tiny, shed-roofed ell—are the secret to fitting two bathrooms into this small laneway house without impinging on the main spaces.

relationship to the end user of the laneway house and see the laneway house (even if it is rented out for a time) as an extension of their home.

Among the quintessential laneway houses Jake and Smallworks have designed and built is a 675-sq.-ft. cottage for a young woman that stands quietly at the back of a corner lot owned by her family. It's a straight-forward, story-and-a-half house, with an open kitchen/dining/living space downstairs and two bedrooms upstairs. There's also a bathroom on each

> *"Some of my inspiration came from catalog houses of the 1920s. . . . The way these houses used space was really smart. There are a lot of lessons to be learned from them."*
>
> —Jake Fry, founder, Smallworks

. . . .

ABOVE AND TOP: It's hard to argue with this time-tested layout for the upstairs of a story-and-a-half house: a bedroom to either side of the stair landing, and a bath in a dormer, straight ahead.

floor. Off the kitchen is a closet with double doors with space for a washer and dryer. Beside the closet is a 40-sq.-ft. storage space that opens to the driveway.

From the laneway, the cottage has an archetypal house shape; it's a refined version of a house a child would draw, and that's a compliment. There's a lot to be said for this honest form, not the least of which is that it fits the neighborhood. Susan's laneway cottage does the fundamental things a house must do, and it does them simply and elegantly, delivering on Jake's promise for Smallworks. III

designer and builder
LANEFAB DESIGN/BUILD

location
**VANCOUVER,
BRITISH COLUMBIA**

live/work laneway house

graphic artist Bambi was looking to build something different at the back of her mother's property in East Vancouver when she called on Bryn Davidson and Mat Turner of the design-build firm Lanefab. She wanted a modern, live/work laneway house designed around her studio. Since privacy wasn't an issue for the workspace, Bryn placed it in a loft, atop a solid form within the vaulted volume of the living space, a kind of box within a box, clad in reclaimed lumber of various patinated colors and hues. The living space consists of a simple sitting area and a cheery kitchen, with three blends of yellow accent tiles fading out as they dance up the wall and a live-edge table on wheels that can be used as a work surface or rolled out for dining. Bambi's bedroom and a bathroom are below the loft, a half-flight down from the main space.

Bambi's mother's house is a postwar Sears house, a small standard-issue rancher. The laneway house is a more expressive structure, although it's just 760 sq. ft. With corrugated steel siding and a shed roof, it has the utilitarian quality of an outbuilding or garage, which feels right at home on a laneway.

Where things get interesting—and more domestic—is on the side of the laneway house that faces the main house, in a shared backyard with

LEFT: The sloping laneway allowed the house to be configured as a split level, with a bedroom and bath below the main level, a loft studio above it, and none of the suburban stigma often attached to the form.

BELOW: Bambi's metal-clad, modernist laneway adds punch to the quiet corner of two perpendicular laneways behind her mother's ranch house.

"Many laneways are leftover spaces used for storage and garbage collection. When a laneway house is introduced, the lane becomes greener, more active, and safer."

—Bryn Davidson, founder, Lanefab

two patios that meet in the middle, separated only by low parapet walls and the three steps up to Bambi's raised patio. To one side of the patio is a rain garden that captures and filters all of the rainwater from the laneway house's roof. Think of the rain garden as a concrete water tank filled with plants and loose rocks that holds water beneath its pervious surface. Water held below grade in the tank can be pumped out for irrigating the garden; excess water flows into the city's storm sewer system, but more slowly than it would without buffering from the rain garden. It's an apt metaphor for laneway houses, which, in their fashion, act as a buffer in Vancouver's superheated housing market. III

· · · ·

FACING PAGE: Without the need for privacy in this laneway house for one, Bambi's graphic-art workspace fits neatly in a loft that's open to the living space below.

ABOVE LEFT: The main living area benefits from a sweeping roof and the flow of space up into the loft studio, an instructive example of volume and openness making up for square footage.

ABOVE RIGHT: The charming kitchen is a study in balance and restraint: a basic layout of plain white cabinets combined with an artful tile treatment and a live-edge table on wheels.

architect
JWT ARCHITECTURE AND PLANNING

builder
VISION BUILT CONSTRUCTION

location
VANCOUVER,
BRITISH COLUMBIA

retreat
within reach

. . . .

ABOVE: Karl and Josefine built this wheelchair-accessible ADU behind the home they own but no longer occupy. After Josefine's stroke, the couple rented out the house and moved to an apartment nearby. The ADU allows them to return to their backyard garden.

LEFT: Unlike most laneway houses, which orient to the laneway, leaving the backyard to the main house, Karl and Josefine's laneway house opens to the backyard garden. Concrete paths make the garden a wheelchair-accessible oasis in the city.

In 1971, a year after Karl and Josefine bought their house in Vancouver's Riley Park neighborhood, Karl built a pond in the backyard for the Japanese-inspired garden that Josefine would tend for decades to come. Fast-forward some 45 years. After a stroke left Josefine with limited mobility, she and Karl moved to an apartment nearby. They rented out their house and put aside long-held dreams of building a getaway cottage somewhere. Until Karl got an idea. What if they built their getaway right in their own backyard? They could stay there during the day when they tired of the apartment, Karl would take a turn as gardener, and they'd have a place to offer to out-of-town family and guests.

Karl had two stipulations for architect James Tuer and builder Tobias Puga: The small house had to be wheelchair accessible, and the garden had to be visible from every window. The garden had become overgrown without Josefine to look after it, so Karl also asked James to work with him to redesign the garden. For the purpose of aging in place, Karl wanted a small, private bedroom for a live-in caregiver, should one be needed at some point. And Karl professed a fondness for Scandinavian modern design.

As the name suggests, a laneway house typically orients to the laneway; the bulk of the backyard is preserved for the main house. But the

211

A weathered cedar fence provides a backdrop to the garden. Thin, horizontal slats allow a peek beyond the fence and fit with the cottage, a blend of Scandinavian modern and Craftsman styles that feels at home in the Pacific Northwest.

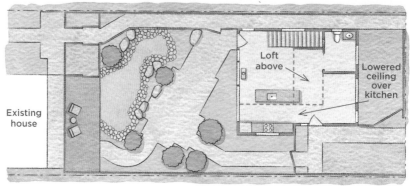

Existing house

Loft above

Lowered ceiling over kitchen

SITE PLAN

• • • •

BELOW: The tall, skylit volume of the interior provides a quality of spaciousness unavailable to Karl and Josefine in their apartment. The room was designed around a wheelchair-accessible kitchen worktable with sink that the couple had already purchased.

essence of Karl's idea was to have a spacious garden with a small cottage set within it. With persistence, James was able to convince the city that, in this case, the garden belonged with the laneway house. Likewise, for privacy, laneway houses typically have few windows facing the backyard and main house. The urban cottage James designed for Karl and Josefine is exactly the opposite; it's all glass facing the garden. It works because the main house has few windows facing the backyard, and because James and Tobias added a structure between the two houses that contains a covered pergola and twin recycling sheds. The structure serves as both a privacy screen and a gateway to the garden and cottage.

Staying within the story-and-a-half height limit for laneway houses, James fit a study and bath under a raised roof; the small suite

• • • •

ABOVE: The daybed can move from its nook to other spots in the room, always with a garden view. A wheelchair-accessible full bath (in the corner) is close at hand. Stairs lead to a study and bath that can convert to quarters for a caregiver if necessary.

RIGHT: A wall of windows extends the interior out to the garden. A clear-glass stair railing and kitchen worktable on legs contribute to the open feel, while a wide, cedar-clad soffit gently shelters and defines the kitchen area.

"The idea was that it would be a retreat, similar to Voltaire's Candide, *retreating in his retirement to tend a garden."*

—Karl, homeowner

• • • •

ABOVE LEFT AND RIGHT: A "thick wall" of cedar-clad recycling sheds and a garden pergola screens the garden from the main house. The covered deck hovers beside a pond and a mugo pine that Karl had placed in the original backyard garden some 45 years previously.

can serve as a caregiver's quarters. Most of the allowable height is given over to a tall section of the open first floor, a vaulted space that adds light and drama to the pared-down interior. The simplicity and openness suit Karl's Scandinavian modern aesthetic, but—equally important—the open space allows for Josefine's wheelchair to be moved freely and for her daybed to be rolled to different spots in the space.

To afford the laneway cottage, Karl and Josefine refinanced their house, which keeps the house in the family. Their two grown children thought this was a great idea. "They and all the kids in the neighborhood have fallen into the pond at least once," Karl says by way of explaining the pull the property has for the next generation.

"For me," Karl says, "just having a little bit of land that I can plant something in is a valuable thing." It's not a selfish wish. The way James sees it, the laneway house is Karl's gift to Josefine. In building it, he has brought her home. ▓

CREDITS

**URBAN CABIN REVISITED
(pp. 124–129)**
ARCHITECT: Robert Swain, Robert
Edson Swain Architecture + Design
PHOTOGRAPHERS: Ken Gutmaker
(p. 124; 126, bottom; 127; 128, top; 129,
left), Ben Benschneider (p. 125), Ken
Wagner (p. 126, top left, top right),
Andrew Ryznar (p. 128, bottom; 129,
center, right)

ONE-ROOM HOUSE (pp. 130–134)
DESIGNER: FUNN ROBERTS
PHOTOGRAPHER: David Tamburo

LIVE/WORK STABLE (pp. 135–139)
ARCHITECTS: Mark Lawrence, Elizabeth
Emerson, EL Studio, New York, NY, and
Washington, DC; www.elstudioarch.com
PHOTOGRAPHER: Mark Lawrence,
EL Studio PLLC

BUNGALOW OPENS UP (pp. 140–144)
DESIGNER: Mark Egerstrom, Mark
Egerstrom Design, West Hollywood,
CA; www.markegerstrom.com
PHOTOGRAPHER: Lisa Romerein/OTTO

COLORFUL COLONIAL (pp. 145–149)
ARCHITECT: David Eisen, FAIA, Abacus
Architects + Planners, Boston, MA;
www.abacusarchitects.com
BUILDER: Paul Morse, Morse
Constructions Inc., Somerville, MA;
www.morseconstructions.com
PHOTOGRAPHER: Morse Constructions
Inc.
ILLUSTRATOR: Christine Erikson,
© The Taunton Press Publishers Inc.

**INDUSTRIAL CONVERSION
(pp. 150–155)**
ARCHITECT: Todd Davis, Todd Davis
Architecture, San Francisco, CA;
td-architecture.com
PHOTOGRAPHER: Mark Luthringer
ILLUSTRATOR: Todd Davis Architecture

FOUND HOME (pp. 156–160)
ARCHITECTS: Brad Zizmor, Dag Folger,
A+I (Architecture Plus Information),
New York, NY; www.aplusi.com
PHOTOGRAPHER: Roland Bello
ILLUSTRATOR: © A+I (Architecture Plus
Information)

SISTERS IN THE CITY (pp. 161–165)
DESIGNER and BUILDER: Kim Clem-
ents, Joe Schneider, J.A.S. Design Build,
Seattle, WA; jasdesignbuild.com
PHOTOGRAPHERS: Jesse Young,
except p. 164 (top) courtesy J.A.S.
Design Build

**ADU ACCESSORY DWELLING
UNIT OPENER (pp. 166–167)**
PHOTOGRAPHER: Ihor Pona

THE BIKE SHED (pp. 168–172)
ARCHITECT: Jack Barnes, Jack
Barnes Architect, Portland, OR;
www.jackbarnesarchitect.com
PHOTOGRAPHERS: Jack Barnes, except
p. 172 Justin and Sarah Schumacher
ILLUSTRATOR: Christine Erikson,
© The Taunton Press Publishers Inc.

SUSAN'S COTTAGE (pp. 173–175)
DESIGNER and BUILDER: Kevin Casey,
New Avenue Homes, Emeryville, CA;
www.newavenuehomes.com
PHOTOGRAPHER: Kevin Casey,
New Avenue Homes
ILLUSTRATOR: Christine Erikson,
© The Taunton Press Publishers Inc.

GARAGE ADU (pp. 176–180)
DESIGNER and BUILDER: Brian Danger,
zenbox design, Portland, OR;
www.zenboxdesign.com
PHOTOGRAPHER: Shauna Intelisano
ILLUSTRATOR: Bryan Danger, zenbox
design

ECO GUEST HOUSE (pp. 181–184)
DESIGNER: Brian Danger, zenbox
design, Portland, OR;
www.zenboxdesign.com
PHOTOGRAPHER: Caitlin Murray at
Built Photo
ILLUSTRATOR: Bryan Danger, zenbox
design

**SHIPPING CONTAINER ADU
(pp. 185–188)**
DESIGNER and BUILDER: Julio Garcia,
Price Street Projects, Hialeah, FL;
pricestreetprojects.com
PHOTOGRAPHER: Courtesy Savannah
College of Art and Design
ILLUSTRATOR: Price Street Projects

**COMPACT BACKYARD COTTAGE
(pp. 189–193)**
DESIGNER: Stephanie Dyer, Dyer
Studio Inc., Portland, OR;
www.dyerstudioinc.com
PHOTOGRAPHER: Dyer Studio Inc.
ILLUSTRATOR: Dyer Studio Inc.

**THREE VANCOUVER LANEWAY
HOUSES**
PHOTOGRAPHERS: Colin Perry/
Lanefab (p. 194, left; 195), Ihor Pona
(p. 194, right)

**CONTEMPORARY LANEWAY HOUSE
(pp. 196–200)**
DESIGNER and BUILDER: Bryn
Davidson, Mat Turner, Lanefab Design/
Build, Vancouver, British Columbia,
Canada; www.lanefab.com
PHOTOGRAPHER: Colin Perry/Lanefab
ILLUSTRATOR: Lanefab Design/Build

LANEWAY CLASSIC (pp. 201–204)
DESIGNER and BUILDER: Jake
Fry, Smallworks, Vancouver, British
Columbia, Canada; www.smallworks.ca
PHOTOGRAPHER: Ihor Pona

**LIVE/WORK LANEWAY HOUSE
(pp. 205–209)**
DESIGNER and BUILDER: Bryn
Davidson, Mat Turner, Lanefab Design/
Build, Vancouver, British Columbia,
Canada; www.lanefab.com
PHOTOGRAPHER: Colin Perry/Lanefab

RETREAT WITHIN REACH (pp. 210–215)
ARCHITECT: James, Tuer, JWT
Architecture and Planning, Bowen
Island, British Columbia, Canada;
jwtarchitecture.com
BUILDER: Vision Built Construction,
Vancouver, British Columbia, Canada;
visionbuilt.ca
PHOTOGRAPHER: Andrew Latreille
ILLUSTRATOR: Christine Erikson,
© The Taunton Press Publishers Inc.